£2

D1650663

WORLD FAMOUS
CRIMES OF
PASSION

Colin Wilson
with Damon and Rowan Wilson

SIENA

This is a Siena Book
Siena is an imprint of Parragon Book Service Ltd
Produced by Magpie Books 1996
First published by Magpie Books,
an imprint of Robinson Publishing Ltd

Robinson Publishing Ltd
7 Kensington Church Court
London W8 4SP

Copyright Robinson Publishing © 1992
Illustrations © Hulton Deutsch
Cover pictures: Amy Robsart, Topham, Mrs Maybrick, Popperfoto.

All rights reserved. No part of this publication may be
reproduced, stored in a retrieval system, or transmitted, in
any form or by any means, electronic, mechanical,
photocopying, recording, or otherwise, without the prior
permission of Robinson Publishers.

ISBN 0 75251 629 9

Printed and Bound in the EC

Contents

Introduction

C*rime passionel* — the crime of passion. The words conjure up dark-skinned southerners like Rudolph Valentino, and sultry girls with daggers concealed in their stockings. "The passion killer is characterized by emotional immaturity and a simplistic moral outlook", said Dr Magnus Hirschfeld, an expert on sex crime. Perhaps this explains why criminologists have paid so little attention to the *crime passionel*. It seems too simple, too straightforward. A hot-tempered man strangles his flirtatious lover. What is there to exercise the ingenuity of a psychologist?

A great deal more than appears on the surface. It *is* true that southerners are more prone to commit crimes of passion than northerners. We say this is because northerners are more cerebral and calculating, while southerners are more hot-blooded and emotional. But in that case, why is the rate of sex crime higher in northern countries? A man who commits murder for the satisfaction of a momentary physical impulse cannot really be called more cerebral or calculating than a man who plans how to kill his mistress' husband.

No, the real explanation is more complicated and more interesting. To begin with, geography and climate play an important part. In northern countries, with their cold and difficult conditions, men and women have tended to develop as equals. They work hard together; and the women, muffled in their winter clothes, do not draw attention to their physical attractions. Perhaps this explains why the Eskimos, according to early travellers, used to offer their wives to the guest. In warmer countries, the difference between male and female is more obvious. The sun-bronzed peasant of Italy or Spain wears his open-necked shirt; the girl wears her brightly-coloured skirt and off-the-shoulder blouse. Sexual maturity comes earlier in the warmer climate. The consequence is that southern men and women see one another as two separate races, almost separate species.

Now when this happens, their view of one another becomes strangely intermingled with illusions and idealizations. Maxim Gorky has caught this with great psychological accuracy in his story *Twenty Six Men and a Girl*. The men are baker's assistants confined all day in a damp cellar and they are all in love with a girl called Tanya who calls there every day. One day, a swaggering soldier tells them that he could seduce Tanya – and he does it. Suddenly the twenty six men hate her; they turn on her and scream insults at her. And Tanya haughtily walks off, never to return. *She* is the realist. The soldier may have treated her like a whore, but he has given her pleasure. These men treat her like an angel, and then abuse her when she fails to live up to it.

Now this tradition – of regarding woman as a romantic goddess – has its roots deep in the southern cultural tradition. The "troubadours" were poets who flourished in southern France and northern Italy as early as the eleventh century, and they invented the tradition of "courtly love". The troubadour's "lady" was his absolute ruler; at a word from her, he would ride off round the world. The stories of King Arthur and his knights of the round table were first written in French, by poets who were inspired by the troubadours and their attitude to women. Scholars believe that the whole tradition of troubadour love originated among the Arabs of north Africa.

There is another – and less pleasant – side to the romantic view of Woman. She is supposed to be quiet, obedient and infinitely yielding. The Italian poet Petrarch told a story that remained popular for centuries. A marquis

2

who distrusts women finally marries a poor peasant girl called Griseldis. Then he proceeds to "test" her to see how obedient she is. First, he takes her children from her as soon as they are born. Then he announces that he intends to divorce in order to marry another woman. Patient Griseldis agrees to everything — even attending his wedding and praising the beauty of the bride-to-be. Finally, overcome by her gentleness and patience, the marquis admits that he has merely been testing her. He takes her back, and "they live happily ever after".

Even if it *is* only a story, it captures the medieval attitude to women in a country like Spain or Italy. To modern ears it sounds sadistic and slightly insane. Surely the marquis could tell that she was a sweet, obedient girl without subjecting her to such humiliations? But that would not have satisfied Petrarch's readers, male or female. For Griseldis was supposed to be their idea of a perfect woman — beautiful, obedient, long-suffering, entirely dependent upon Man, her master.

It is because these deep-rooted attitudes still persist in the southern temperament that southerners are prone to commit crimes of passion. The women who swooned over Rudolph Valentino or John Boles had no idea of what it would really be like to be married to a Sheik. The rape in the desert might be exciting, but the rest could be hell — as Marie Laurent discovered when she married Prince Ali Kamel Bey Fahmy (*see* page 105). But at least it was Prince Fahmy who ended up with three bullets in him. In so many parallel cases it is the woman who dies.

In 1972 Francisco Pineda, a car mechanic of Guadalahara, Mexico, walked into the bedroom of his employer, Fernando Ortega, a thirty-two-year-old hunchback. His employer lay stretched on the floor in his pyjamas, dead. Francisco's pretty stepdaughter Maria Pineda, lay dead on the bed, her skirt around her thighs. Police discovered that both had died of cyanide poisoning: Ortega had forced her to drink cyanide at knife point, then drank it himself. Ortega was suffering from tuberculosis; Maria was acting as his nurse, administering injections. Ortega fell violently in love with her, but she was not attracted to the hunchback. She may have thought that the drink he forced on her contained knockout drops, and that his intention was simply to rape her. In fact, in spite of the position of her dress, Maria had not been sexually molested. Ortega could have raped her before he killed himself; but that was not what he wanted. He loved her, and wanted to join her in death. The tragedy was stupid, pathetic – and typical of the southern temperament. And we can clearly see the southern attitude to women. He adored her, she was his goddess. But she also had to pay with her life for the sin of disobedience to the male.

To the northern, pragmatic way of thinking, there is something absurd about "crimes of passion". It always seems to the northerner that there is a simpler way out. This explains why the Emmett-Dunne case aroused so little interest in England in 1954, although the newspaper-buying public had followed the activities of Heath, Haigh and Christie with rapt attention. Emmet-Dunne was the army sergeant who killed a fellow sergeant with a karate chop, then hanged him to make the death look like suicide: all this in order that he could marry the dead man's widow. The newspapers headlined the murder trial but the British public was apathetic – it was as if they felt that a man must be a bit weak in the head to risk his neck by committing a murder merely in order to marry a woman. Significantly, Emmet-Dunne was an Irishman – a Celt; and, racially speaking the Celts are "southerners".

Chapter One

Elizabethan & 18th Century Crimes of Passion

F our centuries ago, it was quite different. The Elizabethans had an enthusiastic – not to say morbid – interest in crimes of passion, and the Elizabethan dramatists made the most of it. From Shakespeare's Othello to Webster's Duchess of Malfi, you could almost say that the favourite Elizebethan plot was about a husband murdering his wife, or vice versa. But one of the most popular of these bloody tragedies is virtually unknown today, although some scholars believe it was written by Shakespeare; this is the anonymous Arden of Feversham (1592), which was based on a true case that was discussed all over England. It is described by the famous Elizabethan chronicler Raphael Holinshed, who provided Shakespeare with so many of his plots.

The Murder of Thomas Arden

T homas Arden was a Kentish gentleman, the Mayor of Faversham, who married Alice North, the sister of the North who translated Plutarch. Arden was more interested in money than sex, and Holinshed suggests that he married Alice for her powerful family connections rather than because he was in love with her. Probably her dowry was generous. And having secured her, he went back to his main business of accumulating money and land – he managed to defraud a man named Greene of some abbey lands by using his influence to get a Chancery grant of them. Alice now met a tailor called Thomas Morsby (or Mosbie, as it is spelt in the play) and became his mistress; Morsby was in the service of her father, Sir Edward North. Arden was perfectly happy about handing over his marital duties to Morsby. He invited Morsby to come and live in his house, and left him there to console Alice when he had to go on business trips. He certainly knew what was going on; there was an occasion when he saw Alice with her arms around Morsby's neck, and heard them referring to him as a cuckold. What pleased him less was the discovery that the couple were thinking of murdering him; however, he didn't take this too seriously, and continued to encourage Morsby to keep up the good work. Presumably this left Morsby too tired to do the murder himself; for he approached Greene – the man who has been defrauded – and Greene, in turn,

The murder of Thomas Arden in 1550.

hired two assassins with the beautiful names of Black Will and Shagbag. These proved to be a pair of incompetents, and Charlie Chaplin could have made a superb comedy out of their attempts to kill Arden. Even Shakespeare — or whoever dramatized the case — has a preposterously funny scene in which the two murderers wait for Arden by a market stall, and the stall-keeper swings his shutter into place and cracks the skull of Black Will.

Morsby tried various sophisticated and over-subtle methods of killing Arden — a poisoned crucifix, poisoned pictures, etc — but finally, they were forced to summon Black Will and Shagbag to the house to kill Arden as he sat at table. Morsby finished him off with a blow on the head from a flat iron, after he had been stabbed and throttled. They then dragged the body to a nearby field. It was snowing, so the footprints were obvious, and one of the accomplices forgot to throw the bloodstained knife and towel into the well. The law took violent retribution. Murder of a husband by his wife was regarded as a form of treason, and the penalty was to be burned alive. The servants who had helped in disposing of the body were also tried. Shagbag, Greene and the painter who had supplied poisons managed to escape; the last lines of the play mention that Shagbag was murdered in Southwark. The law was so anxious to make an example of everyone concerned in the murder that an innocent servant named Bradshaw was tried with the others, and sentenced to death, although the rest of the conspirators all asserted that he was not concerned. "These condemned persons were diversely executed in sundry places," says Holinshed; the servant Michael hung in chains at Faversham; a maid servant who had been an accessory was burnt alive, "crying out on hir mistresse that had brought hir to this ende". Morsby and his sister were hanged at Smithfield in London; Alice Arden was burnt at Canterbury on 14 March, and Black Will was also burnt on a scaffold at "Flishing in Zeland". Greene —

the man who had procured the murderers – returned some years later, and was promptly executed and hung in chains. Even a man named Adam Foule, who had merely acted as Alice's messenger to Morsby, was sent to London with his legs tied under the horse's belly and imprisoned in the Marshalsea. Holinshed adds the legend that the imprint of Arden's body could be seen in the grass for many years afterwards; he also notes that Arden had stolen the field in which his corpse was found, from a poor widow. The archives of Canterbury contain the entry: "For the charges of brenning Mistress Arden and execution of George Bradshaw [the innocent servant], 43 shillings."

The play itself is remarkably successful as drama; but it can hardly be called a realistic presentation of the case. Arden – who was obviously a vicious miser – is portrayed as a doting husband who loves his wife so much that he closes his eyes to her infidelities. Alice is made to repent fulsomely when she sees her husband's body; in fact, it was Alice who accused the innocent Bradshaw – hardly the act of a repentant woman.

In short, it is necessary to read between the lines to get the facts of the case. Arden married Alice for money, and then deliberately found her a lover. Alice was almost certainly a nymphomaniac. Why did she accuse Bradshaw, whom the others declared to be innocent? Was it because she had made advances to him and had been rejected? Why was Adam Foule imprisoned, although he had been only a messenger? Was it because the judges suspected that any male connected with Alice might have been her lover?

We also learn something of the Elizabethans from the fate of the maid, who had been merely an accessory after the fact. She was burned alive, while Morsby, the instigator, was only hanged. Why such severity over the murder of a highly unpleasant miser? It is surely a reasonable inference that it was the sexual aspect of the case that aroused this universal morbid interest. The Elizabethan public was very like the public of today, except that it was far less sophisticated, since there were no sensational newspapers to spread the details of every divorce case. There is an immense reservoir of sexual frustration under the surface of working class life, and this case offered it an outlet. Alice Arden was one of these upper class women who spend their days in the arms of lovers; probably every woman in the case was somebody or other's mistress . . . They all deserved burning. So when the story was made into a play, Arden had to be whitewashed — otherwise the sexual motive was made less important, and nobody wanted that . . .

The Mystery of Amy Robsart

Queen Elizabeth I herself may have been party to a murder. Her lover, Sir Robert Dudley, (later the Earl of Leicester), was an extremely handsome but thoroughly spoilt and undisciplined character. When he was only seventeen, he had married Amy Robsart, the daughter of Sir John Robsart, a Norfolk squire — apparently they married for love, and remained in love for some years. But Dudley became involved in the conspiracy to make Lady Jane Grey queen of England. It failed, and Dudley's father, the Earl of Warwick, was executed for his part in it. Dudley was also sentenced to death, and his wife had to visit him in the Tower of London. However, he was pardoned, and redeemed himself by fighting against the French at the Battle of St Quentin (1557). When Elizabeth came to the throne in the following year, Dudley lost no time in hurrying to court, where the twenty-five-year-old queen became violently infatuated with him. Soon he had been appointed Master of the Queen's Horse and made a Knight of the Garter. The

Crimes of Passion

Spanish Ambassador wrote to Philip of Spain to tell him that Robert Dudley would probably be king in the near future.

Two years later, in 1560, the Dudleys moved to Cumnor Place, near Abingdon, Oxfordshire. On 4 September of that year, Queen Elizabeth told a foreign envoy that Amy Robsart was dying — an odd statement in view of the fact that she seems to have been in normal health, and apparently on excellent terms with her husband.

Four days later, on 8 September, 1560, Amy is said to have sent all the servants to Abingdon Fair — her husband was at court. When they returned, they found her body at the foot of the stairs with a fractured skull. Apparently she had slipped on the stairs. The coroner's jury found her death to be accidental. And as the relations between Robert Dudley and the Queen became closer, rumours abounded that Dudley had had his wife murdered, with the Queen's connivance. The actual killer was rumoured to be Sir Anthony Forster, Dudley's Comptroller of the Household at Cumnor, in association with his mistress, Mrs Oddingsells.

For whatever reason, the Queen decided not to marry Dudley. He was probably her lover anyway (although historians deny this), and she had no desire to share power with a husband. She even tried to marry Dudley off to Mary Queen of Scots, but he declined. In 1564, Dudley was created Earl of Leicester.

In 1575, Dudley laid on the famous entertainment for the Queen at Kenilworth Castle, an entertainment described at length by Sir Walter Scott in his novel of that name. The eleven-year-old Shakespeare is said to have witnessed it. But Scott goes on to take some major liberties with English history. He makes Dudley marry Amy secretly, and a villain called Varney later arranges her murder by means of a booby trap outside her bedroom door.

Was Amy murdered? The historian Ian Aird argues that her death was an accident, due to the cancer of the breast

The great Elizabethan scandal was the murder in the Tower of London of Sir Thomas Overbury – a murder that involved adultery, poison and homosexuality.

King James the First, who succeeded Queen Elizabeth in 1603, was a homosexual. In 1606, while the king was watching a tournament, a page named Robert Carr broke his leg. A tall, good-looking young man, he was soon enjoying the king's favour.

Carr was already involved with another homosexual, Thomas Overbury, eleven years his senior. Overbury now became Carr's secretary, reading the king's mail and secret dispatches.

In 1610, the beautiful fifteen-year-old Frances Howard, daughter of the Earl of Suffolk, came to court. She was already the wife of the teenage Earl of Essex – an arranged marriage which had not yet been consummated. It was Carr who consummated it. When the husband returned from France and took her to the country, she refused to grant him his marital rights. Eventually, the Archbishop of Canterbury was persuaded to grant a divorce.

Overbury became frantic at the thought of Carr marrying Frances Howard; he made so much fuss that the king had him thrown in the Tower.

There Frances arranged to have him poisoned, with the connivance of the Governor of the Tower, Sir Gervase Elwes. On 15 September, 1613, Overbury died after five months of agony.

Eighteen months after Carr married Frances, the chemist's assistant who had administered the final dose of mercuric sublimate made a deathbed confession. Elwes and three accomplices were put on trial and executed in the autumn of 1615. Carr and his wife were tried in the following year and both sentenced to death. Confined in the Tower for six years, they were then allowed to return to their country home. But love had turned to hatred; they never spoke to one another. Frances died of a disease of the womb at the age of thirty-nine; Carr lived on gloomily for many years more; when he went to see the king, James broke down and cried on his shoulder.

from which she is known to have been suffering. But the Simancas Archives indicate that there was a plot to poison Amy, and this may be what the Queen had in mind when she said that Amy was dying. On the other hand, she may merely have known about the cancer of the breast.

Dudley's future career was not particularly glorious, but at least he escaped execution – the fate of Elizabeth's other favourite, the Earl of Essex. When the English went to help the Dutch against the Spanish in 1586, Dudley proved arrogant and incompetent as their commander, and returned home in virtual disgrace. But he had one more triumph – he stage-managed the Queen's famous visit to her troops at Tilbury – when the Spanish Armada was on its way – when she made her famous speech describing herself as "a weak and feeble woman", but with "the heart and stomach of a king". A few months later, in August 1588, Dudley was dead, at the age of fifty-five, of a "burning fever".

Whether or not Dudley planned the murder of his wife, there seems no doubt that he was one of the most unpleasant and treacherous characters in English history.

When Mary Queen of Scots was in prison in 1587, Dudley tried to persuade the Queen to have her quietly poisoned. And with the evidence of a poison plot against Amy in the Simanca Archive, it seems more than likely that her death was no accident.

Catherine Hayes

In 1725, another case of husband-murder created the same kind of nationwide sensation as the Arden of Faversham case. The sheer gruesomeness of the murder, and the fact that the murderess had had several lovers, again titillated the morbid sexuality of the British public, and contributed to making the loose-living lady an almost legendary villainess.

Catherine Hayes was born Catherine Hall, in Birmingham, the daughter of poor parents. In 1705, when she was fifteen, she was noticed by some army officers, who persuaded her to return to their quarters; there she became their collective mistress for a while, until they moved on. She then found a job as a servant with a Warwickshire farmer named Hayes. The son of the house, a carpenter, fell in love with her; one morning, they went secretly into Worcester, and were married. John Hayes was then twenty-one. After six years in the country, his young bride began to dream of London, and persuaded her husband to move there. She was so excitable and quarrelsome that her in-laws raised no objection. In London, John Hayes became a successful coal merchant, pawnbroker and moneylender. His success in this latter occupation lends colour to his wife's assertion that he was unbearably mean. At all events, Hayes was successful in business, and in a little over ten years, made enough money to sell his shop in the Tyburn Road and take lodgings nearby. His relations with his wife had deteriorated badly. This may have been due to his meanness and her desire for luxury, or there may have been deeper causes. She later told one of her accomplices in the murder that Hayes had murdered two of his children in the country – presumably when they were newborn. *If* Hayes was pathologically mean, there might just possibly be some truth in this story.

Early in 1725, a young man named Thomas Billings, a tailor, came to their house, and Catherine Hayes declared him to be an old friend, or relative. He stayed with them, and when Hayes went to the country on business, Billings took his place in Catherine's bed. The two lovers made the most of their freedom, throwing parties and spending a great deal of the money that Hayes had taken so long to accumulate. When Hayes returned, he was furious, and gave his wife a beating. But for some reason, he did not turn Billings out of the house.

Another friend from Warwickshire now arrived, a Thomas Wood. It was to him that she told the story of her husband killing her two children, and she mentioned that Hayes had also killed a man. Wood also became her lover, and her promise that her husband's estate – some fifteen hundred pounds, a fortune for those days – would be put at his disposal when she became a widow finally made him agree to help her kill her husband.

On 1 March 1725, Wood came back from a visit to the country, and found Billings, Catherine and John Hayes in the midst of a drinking session. Wood, who was young and boastful, declared that he had just drunk a guinea's worth of wine and was still sober, and Billings challenged Hayes to drink the same amount – six bottles. If Hayes could do it without getting drunk, Billings would buy the wine; if not, Hayes should pay for it. Hayes accepted the offer; perhaps the prospect of six bottles of free wine was too much for his miserly soul. Billings, Wood and Catherine Hayes set off for a tavern in New Bond Street, and on the way, she pointed

Catherine Hayes.

out that this would be a good opportunity to kill her husband.

In the Brawn's Head the three of them drank a pint of "best mountain wine", and asked for six pints to be sent up to their lodgings. Catherine Hayes paid 10s 6d for it — perhaps its quality was only half as good as the stuff Wood claimed he had been drinking.

Hayes downed the six pints of wine without much trouble, while the other three drank beer; his wife quietly sent out for another pint which Hayes, now too fuddled to count the bottles, also drank. He then fell down on the floor, woke up after a few minutes, and staggered off to bed in the next room. The bed was probably the kind that Hogarth portrayed, with its lower end actually on the floor. Hayes fell asleep on his face. Billings came in with a coal hatchet, and hit him on the back of the head with it. The blow fractured his skull, and Hayes began to kick his feet in agony, making such a noise that the woman in the room overhead came down to investigate. By this time, Wood had seized the hatchet and given Hayes two more blows, which completed the work of killing him. When Mrs Springate complained that the thudding noise had awakened them, Catherine Hayes explained that her husband had some noisy guests, but that they were about to leave. It must have been a tense moment, and both Wood and Billings were badly unnerved.

The next problem was what to do with the body. They had to get it down two flights of stairs to the street. Then suppose they bumped into a member of the watch? As soon as Hayes was recognized, they were done for. But Catherine Hayes refused to be panicked. She pointed out that if they cut off her husband's head, and disposed of that first, the body would not be identifiable, even if they had to flee from the watch and leave it in the street.

The two men were already nauseated. The bed was drenched with blood; blood had even shot up to the ceiling with the hatchet blows. Catherine Hayes suggested that they decapitate her husband with his neck over a bucket to catch the blood. The two men must have been wishing that this business had never started; but there was obviously no way out except to dispose of the body. So they placed the body on the bed so the head hung over. Catherine Hayes held the bucket underneath the neck, Billings twisted his fingers in the blood-soaked hair, and Woods sawed away at the neck with a carving knife — hatchet blows would have brought Mrs Springate down again. When the head was off, they dropped it in the pail, and left the headless body to bleed into it.

Catherine Hayes recognized that there was still danger. If the head was identified, it would be traced back to her. She proposed boiling it in a pot until the flesh came away — a revolting but sensible idea — but the others were too nervous. They became even more nervous when Mrs Springate shouted down irritably to know what was going on. Here Catherine Hayes showed a presence of mind that entitles her to be ranked with Alice Arden and Lady Macbeth; she called back that her husband had been suddenly called away on a journey, and was getting ready to go. Now the two Thomases could hardly wait to get out of the house. They poured the blood from the bucket down the sink, then had to tiptoe up and down the stairs half a dozen times to get water from the well to wash it down. When that was done, the men crept downstairs, one of them holding the bucket under his coat, while Catherine Hayes walked down behind them, talking in her normal voice, saying goodbye to her husband, in case any of the neighbours was listening. According to the sharp-eared Mrs Springate, she put up an excellent and convincing performance. Then the two men made off as fast as they could, and Catherine Hayes hurried upstairs to clean up the blood before it clotted. It was a long task, because the unpolished floorboards had soaked up the blood like a sponge; even when she had washed it and scraped it with a knife, the marks were still visible.

Meanwhile, Billings and Wood hastened towards the river – a long walk, from the present day Oxford Street down to Whitehall. It was nearly midnight. People of that time tended to go to bed early, and the watch were likely to challenge people who were out after midnight. Billings must have looked as if he was pregnant, with the pail under his greatcoat. They reached Whitehall, but the dock gates had already been closed. The tide was out, and the foreshore of the river was mostly mud; wading across that would attract attention. They walked on along the river, past Westminster, to the Horseferry wharf – at the end of the present Horseferry Road, under Lambeth Bridge. They went to the end of the dock, and threw the head over. Instead of a splash, there was a thud as it landed on mud. But they were too frightened to worry. They threw the bucket after it, and hurried away. The nightwatchman on the wharf heard the thud, and a man on board a boat saw them throw the bucket; but it was a dark night, and no one was very curious. Billings and Wood hastened back home, now feeling slightly better. They found Catherine Hayes still scraping at the floorboards, trying not to make too much noise. The headless body still lay across the bed. The two men made up a makeshift bed in the other room, and tried to sleep. Catherine Hayes sat by them, brooding. She must have been wishing that they had disfigured the face with a knife to prevent recognition. But with luck, the head was already on its way out to sea . . . She was still sitting there when the two men woke up at dawn.

And also at dawn, the nightwatchman, a Mr Robinson, walked to the edge of the dock to stretch his legs, and saw the bucket and the head lying in the mud. A small crowd soon gathered, and the lighterman from the boat mentioned seeing a man throwing the bucket into the river.

Back in the lodgings, the murderers were discussing what to do with the body. The first and most obvious thing was to conceal it in case someone came into the room. Mrs Hayes went out and got a large box; but it was not big enough. They cut off the arms, and the legs at the knees; but the body was still too long. They hacked off the thighs, and finally managed to pack most of the pieces into the box, leaving some of the smaller items in an old blanket. That evening, at 9 o'clock, Wood and Billings crept downstairs with the trunk in a blanket. It was early and there were too many people about; but they were not going to risk being stopped by the watch. This time they went north — fortunately there was not far to go before they were in the fields of Marylebone. They tossed the trunk into a pond that Wood had located during the day, then went back and collected the rest of the body. It was Mrs Springate who let them in at midnight; fortunately, she had no reason to be suspicious, even though her husband had found clots of blood in the drain that morning. Blood was common enough.

The next day, Wood made off to the country to soothe his shattered nerves. Billings resumed his place in his mistress's bed.

The parish officers of Westminster had not been idle. They ordered the blood and dirt to be washed from the head and — a macabre touch — the hair to be combed. Then the head was set on a stake at St Margaret's churchyard in Westminster. It drew a fascinated crowd, but no one recognized it. But the next day, a young apprentice named Bennett saw it, and flew to tell Catherine Hayes that he thought it looked like her husband. She told him angrily that he could get himself into serious trouble if he spread such reports — her husband was alive and well. Bennett apologized and promised to say nothing about it. And a Mr Patrick also thought he recognized the head, and went along to a pub called the Dog and Dial in Monmouth Street

The head of John Hayes, murdered by his wife, was mounted on a pole in Westminster for the purpose of identification.

— at which Hayes and his wife used to drink — to mention his suspicion. Billings happened to be working there at the time, and someone replied that the head couldn't belong to John Hayes, because Billings was his lodger, and he would know if anything had happened to Hayes. Billings immediately confirmed this, saying that he had left Hayes in bed that morning.

Mrs Hayes must have been feeling nervous; but she recognized that flight would be a mistake. When a neighbour asked after her husband, she said he was out taking a walk; the visitor mentioned the head in the churchyard, and Mrs Hayes expressed horror at the wickedness of the age. "Why, they even say they've found bits of a woman's body in a pond at Marylebone," she declared, and the neighbour said she hadn't heard about that.

Wood came back to town on the 5th — two days after he had fled. Catherine Hayes gave him some of her husband's clothes, and five shillings. She told him that the head had been found, but that no one had yet identified it.

The head was beginning to stink; worse still, the features were already beginning to turn black. The parish officers had it placed in a large jar full of spirit — perhaps gin — and continued to exhibit it to anyone who was interested. For a short period it looked as if the mystery was solved when a woman said she thought it was her husband; but after a long look at it, she said she couldn't swear to it.

Catherine Hayes remained remarkably cool. Less than a week after the murder, she left her lodgings and moved to another in the neighbourhood, taking Billings, Wood, and Mrs Springate. No doubt she was afraid that the latter might gossip; she even paid a quarter's rent for the lady. She then proceeded to collect as many of her husband's debts as possible, even threatening to sue her husband's brother-in-law for money he owed. She wrote various letters in her husband's name to other debtors.

Crimes of Passion

Inevitably, Hayes' friends began to wonder what had become of him. A man called Ashby called on her to enquire. She then told him, in strict confidence, that her husband had killed a man in a quarrel, and had fled to Portugal. Mr Ashby asked if the head found in the river belonged to the murdered man, but Mrs Hayes said no, they had buried the body entire.

All this was bound to arouse suspicion. Ashby communicated with the neighbour who had already enquired; they talked with another neighbour. And finally, a Justice of the Peace was informed. They hurried to Catherine Hayes' lodgings and knocked on the door. She was in bed with Billings; she dressed and went to the door. Billings was sitting on the edge of the bed without shoes or stockings when the officers came in. When asked if he had been sleeping with her, she said no, he was mending his stockings. The Justice remarked that he must have been doing it in the dark, since there was no candle or fire.

Wood was not present, but they arrested Catherine Hayes, Billings and Mrs Springate, and took them off to different prisons, to prevent them concocting a story. Catherine Hayes continued to assert her innocence, and asked if she might see the head from the churchyard. The Justice agreed, and they took her to the barber-surgeon – a Mr Westbrook – who was keeping the head. Here, Catherine Hayes called upon all her histrionic powers, and shouted: "Oh, it is my dear husband's head!" and proceeded to kiss the jar. Mr Westbrook came in and said he would take the head out of the jar – it was generally believed in those days that murderers would reveal their guilt if forced to touch the corpse. But Catherine Hayes was equal to anything; she seized the head and kissed it, then asked if she could have a lock of its hair. Her performance must have been a little too dramatic; the barber-surgeon replied sardonically that she had already had too much of his blood; at which Catherine Hayes fainted, or pretended to. She had already run through the emotional spectrum; it was the only thing left for her to do.

While all this was taking place, someone saw the blanket floating in the Marylebone pond, and pulled it out. The rest of the body was soon recovered. But Catherine Hayes and Thomas Billings continued to assert their total innocence.

Wood was the weak link in the chain. On the following Sunday, he came back to London from Harrow, and went along to Catherine Hayes' old lodgings. They told him she had moved to a house nearby, and someone offered to show him. His informant took him to the wrong place — to the house of Mr Longmore, one of the neighbours who had caused the arrest. There the terrified Wood was dragged off his horse, and taken to the Justice who had been questioning the others. At first, Wood declared himself innocent; but in Newgate, his nerve broke, and he made a full confession. He explained that Mrs Hayes had told him that her husband was an atheist and freethinker, and that "it would be no more sin to kill him than to kill a dog". When the other two were told of the confession, they decided that there was no further point in keeping silent — especially as it might lead to torture — and also confessed. Mrs Springate was released.

It was after this that Catherine Hayes suddenly realized that the charge against her was not of murder, but petty treason — the killing of her lord and master; and that the penalty for this was to be burned alive. But she still hoped that her crime might be regarded simply as murder, since she had not struck any of the blows that killed her husband. At her trial, with the fear of a painful death hanging over her, she denied that she had any hand in the actual killing of her husband, and said that she had kept silent only because she was afraid that Wood and Billings would kill her too. When it was clear that all three would be sentenced to death, Wood and Billings begged that they might not be hanged in chains, and she again repeated her plea to be

Catherine Hayes burned at the stake for murder.

hanged rather than burned. But the judge sentenced her to be burned, and she screamed all the way back to Newgate.

She revealed a better side to her nature before her execution; she sent messages to her two ex-lovers, regretting that she had involved them in all this. When she saw Billings in chapel, she sat holding his hand and leaned her head on his shoulder. She was obviously in love with Billings.

A few days before her execution, she somehow managed to get a bottle of acid into her cell. Unfortunately, a fellow prisoner saw it and tasted it. A little spilt on a handkerchief burnt it. So the prisoner smashed the bottle on the floor.

Wood caught a fever in prison, and died before he could be executed. He is the only person in the case who seems to deserve much sympathy. His age is not recorded, but it seems fairly certain that he was still in his teens. He seems to have been a good-natured, easy-going young man who was too easily influenced.

Billings was also young. Osborn records that when he first came to stay at the Hayes' lodgings, there was a rumour that he was Catherine Hayes' son by a previous "connection". He was executed before Catherine Hayes, and when the executioner — Richard Arnet, Laughing Jack's predecessor — came to fetch her, she asked him if he had killed her "dear child" yet.

Her last moments give the case a final touch of horror. It was customary to strangle a woman condemned for petty treason before burning her. Arnet lit the brushwood around her, then started to pull the strangling rope from behind; but the fire reached his hands too quickly, and he had to let go. The spectators watched her trying to push the burning faggots away while she screamed. More faggots were thrown on, to try to put her out of her misery soon, "but", says Wilkinson, "she survived amidst the flames for a considerable time, and her body was not perfectly reduced to ashes in less than three hours".

Chapter Two

The Use of
Poisons

T he violent method chosen by Catherine Hayes to despatch
her husband has few parallels among crimes of passion.
Most women who wished to get rid of an unwanted spouse chose
poison. Not only was it likely to attract less attention; it had the
enormous additional advantage of being practically undetectable.
Science had not yet invented a sure method of identifying poisons
once they were in the human system. And even before they entered
the human system, the usual method of testing them was to try
them on a dog or cat, and see if the animal went into convulsions.

The Affair of the Poisons

W hile the English remained rigidly puritanical in the
matter of extramarital love affairs, the attitude of
the French was altogether more lax. This was never more
true than at the court of the Sun King, Louis the Fourteenth,
where a wife without a lover was even rarer than a husband
without a mistress. In most cases, both spouses accepted the
situation with good humoured tolerance. But there were
inevitably a few cases where the husband or wife decided
that a permanent change of partner would be desirable, and
that murder would solve the problem more conveniently
than divorce. In 1673, the thirtieth year of Louis's reign,
such deaths reached epidemic proportions.

It was in that year that Nicholas de la Reynie, Louis's Chief of Police, was informed by two priests that many penitents were asking absolution for poisoning their spouses. A young lawyer who was having dinner with a fortune-teller known as La Vigoreux, wife of a tailor, was startled to hear another fortune-teller, Marie Bosse, declare: "What a marvellous trade! Duchesses, marquises, princes! Three more poisonings and I'll be able to retire." The lawyer passed on this information to Desgrais, who sent the wife of one of his officers along to ask Marie Bosse's advice about her husband's cruelty. On the second visit, Mme Bosse handed over a phial of a colourless poison, together with precise instructions for using it. And finally, on 4 January 1669, the police descended on Marie Bosse in the early hours of the morning and placed her under arrest. La Reynie was shocked to be told that Marie had been found sharing a huge bed with her two sons and her daughters, for it was believed that magical powers could be passed from one member of a family to another by incest. La Vigoreux was also arrested, and she and Bosse proved more than willing to talk. At first, La Reynie thought he was dealing with a harmless matter of witch-craft — love potions and magic spells — for although belief in magic was still common among the uneducated class, the aristocracy of the Age of Reason was already inclined to dismiss it as pure imagination. But as La Reynie listened to the confessions, he realized with alarm that Marie Bosse had not been exaggerating when she talked about her clients: this affair involved the "highest in the land". Moreover, Bosse and La Vigoreux were associated with an eminent fortune-teller called Catherine Deshayes, known as La Voisin, whose wealthy and aristocratic clients included members of the court. One client, Mme de Poulaillon, was the wife of the Master of Forests and Waterways in Champagne, while another two, Mme Leféron and Mme Dreux, were the wives of Paris magistrates who would probably be called to try these "witches". Finally, with astonishment, La Reynie heard the names of two of the king's mistresses, Louise de la Vallière and Mme de Montespan, and at that point he knew that the king himself must be informed. And when the king heard the details, he decided immediately that this could not be tried in open court; all this talk of poisons and love potions could only bring the monarchy into discredit. La Vigoreux was tortured — she died under torture — and so were Marie Bosse and La Voisin. They told amazing stories of poison and magic spells. The pretty Mme Poulaillon, burdened with an ageing husband and a demanding lover, had been given shirts treated with arsenic, which would cause her husband to scratch himself, and a "healing ointment" that would kill him in ten weeks. But her husband had come to suspect her designs, and had her confined in a convent. And Mme de Montespan, for ten years the king's favourite mistress, had called on the sorceresses whenever the king's affections had seemed to be diminishing, and had been supplied with love potions and aphrodisiacs, including Spanish fly, mashed blister beetles, cocks' combs and cocks' testicles. And there was worse to come. Montespan had raised the question of whether the queen and Louise de la Vallière might be killed by witchcraft. This was beyond the powers of the fortune-tellers; they sent her instead to the "high priest of devil worship", an evil old man called Abbé Guibourg. The essence of the black masses performed by Guibourg was the sacrifice of a newborn baby. Mme de Montespan was made to lie naked on a bed, her feet dangling on the floor, with the sacred chalice on her groin. La Voisin brought in a baby, and Guibourg slit its throat over the chalice, into which he drained its blood, reciting the names of Mme de Montespan and the king. The child's entrails were removed, and its body burned in a furnace; the entrails were used for distilling a magic potion — which included the Host used in the black mass —

and this was given to Mme de Montespan to administer to the king.

La Voisin's daughter, who described all this, also told how a lady of the court named Mme des Oeillets had come for a magic potion, accompanied by a man; Guibourg had explained that he would need to mix the sexual discharges of both into the potion. But since Mme des Oeillets was menstruating, he accepted instead some of her menstrual blood, which he mixed with the sperm which the man had produced by masturbating into the chalice.

The king was horrified. If this became known, he would be the laughing stock of Europe. He therefore gave orders that the case should be tried in private. The trial began in April 1679, and dragged on until July 1683; 104 defendants appeared before a selected panel of twelve judges in a chamber of the old Paris Arsenal; since this was lit by candles and torches it became known as the Chambre Ardente (lighted chamber). Many other priests were found to be involved, and the king was shocked to discover the astonishing extent of black magic in France. Thirty-six death sentences were handed out, and four life sentences to the galleys; another thirty-four prisoners were sentenced to banishment or heavy fines. No word of the proceedings leaked outside the walls of the "Poison Chamber", but the long and grim series of executions left the public in no doubt of the seriousness of the crimes involved. The name of Mme de Montespan was never mentioned; she had been replaced by a new favourite, Mme de Maintenon – who had been her protégé – and retired to a convent. In 1709, the king ordered that all papers relating to the case should be destroyed; but by some error, the minute-book of the clerk of the court was overlooked; it was finally published in the second half of the nineteenth century, revealing for the first time one of the most incredible stories of murder and black magic in the recorded annals of crime.

Mary Blandy

The first poisoning case in which medical evidence played the decisive role was the trial, in 1751, of Mary Blandy, charged with poisoning her father with arsenic. In 1746, at the age of twenty-six, Mary was still unmarried, although she was an heiress to a fortune of £10,000; her father, a prosperous lawyer of Henley-on-Thames, took exception to most of the young men who showed signs of interest in his plain but good-natured daughter. But in that year, Mary made the acquaintance of a Scottish captain, the Honourable William Henry Cranstoun, who immediately began to pay her attentions. Cranstoun had many disadvantages; he was small, pock-marked, cross-eyed, and already married; none of this prevented him from deciding to win Mary's hand. The first step was to rid himself of his wife, who was being supported by her relatives in Scotland. He wrote to her explaining that his chances of advancement in the army were poor while he was married, and begging her to write him a letter stating that she had merely been his mistress. She was finally persuaded to do this, whereupon Cranstoun circulated copies to his and her relatives, and instituted divorce proceedings. His wife opposed it and proved that their marriage was legal. And Mr Blandy, who had been prepared to accept Cranstoun as a son-in-law – after all, he was the brother of a Scottish peer – indignantly reproached the ugly little Scot and indicated that the engagement was at an end. Cranstoun nevertheless continued to call, and he and Mary continued to regard themselves as secretly engaged, although she declined his suggestion that they should run away and marry. Mrs Blandy became the captain's ardent ally after he had given her £40 to pay a debt she had contracted on a visit to London. Soon after this visit, in September 1749, Mrs Blandy became suddenly ill and died, begging her husband to allow Mary to marry Cranstoun. When Cranstoun wrote to Mary, telling her that

Mary Blandy, hanged for murder in 1752.

he was besieged by the bailiffs, and needed his £40, she borrowed the money and sent it to him.

From this point on, we must accept either the version of those who believe Mary guilty, or those who are convinced she was an innocent dupe. Cranstoun explained to her that he knew a fortune-teller called Mrs Morgan, whose magic potions could be relied upon to make her father change his mind. And on a visit to the Blandy household in 1750, Cranstoun apparently demonstrated the efficacy of a magic powder by slipping some of it into the old gentleman's tea. He had been in the worst of tempers at breakfast, yet overflowing with benevolence at dinner. Mary allowed herself to be persuaded to continue the doses. And in April 1751, Cranstoun sent Mary some "Scotch pebbles" — a fashionable ornament at the time — together with a white powder for cleaning them. Mary began to administer the powder to her father in small doses. And the fact that Francis Blandy began to suffer acute stomach pains must have made her aware that the potion was less harmless than her lover claimed. And when the servant, Susan Gunnel, tasted some of the gruel that Mr Blandy was about to eat, she also became ill. After that, Susan poured out the gruel from the pan and noticed a gritty white powder in the bottom; she took this to a neighbour, who sent it to an apothecary. But since no reliable chemical test was known for arsenic, no immediate analysis was attempted. Nevertheless, Susan went to Mr Blandy and warned him that she thought he was being poisoned by his own daughter. And when Blandy asked Mary if she had put anything into his tea, she became pale, and hurried from the room.

Incredibly, Mr Blandy took no steps to prevent Mary from meddling with his food. And when he was shown a letter Mary had written to Cranstoun, begging him to take care of what he wrote, he only smiled and said: "Poor lovesick girl! What a woman will do for the man she loves." Then he continue to sink. And when Mary, now in a panic, threw some letters and powder into the kitchen fire, the cook rescued the powder as soon as she left the room. Mr Blandy asked to see Mary, who fell on her knees and begged him not to curse her; he told her that he blessed her, and hoped God would forgive her. Two days later, he died.

That same afternoon, Mary begged the footman to accompany her to France, and offered him £500, which he refused. The following morning, she ran out of the house and tried to escape, but was soon surrounded by an angry crowd. Her lover was more successful; when he heard news of her arrest, he fled to France.

When Mary was tried, on 3 March 1752, the main witnesses against her were four doctors. They agreed that the condition of Mr Blandy's inner organs suggested arsenic poisoning, and that the white powder they had analysed was arsenic. But the only test they had been able to apply involved touching a red-hot iron to the powder, and sniffing the vapour, which they declared to be that of arsenic. In later years such evidence would have been unhesitatingly rejected. On the other hand, servants were able to state, in considerable detail, when and how Mary had administered poison to her father – to such an extent that it now seems astonishing that Mr Blandy was not warned in time. Mary made a passionate speech in which she flatly denied administering poison although she admitted that she *had* put a powder into her father's food "which had been given me with another intent". She gave her father the powder, she said, to make him fond of Cranstoun. The prosecution rejected this with contempt, pointing out that she had attempted to destroy the powder as soon as she knew she was suspected. And after thirteen hours, the jury took only five minutes to find Mary guilty.

Six weeks later, her hands bound with black ribbon, she mounted the gallows outside Newgate, insisting to the end that she had no intention of killing her father. Her last words were to ask the hangman not to hang her too high "for the sake of decency". Cranstoun survived her by only six months, dying "in considerable agony" at Furnes, in Flanders, in his fortieth year.

Where Cranstoun was concerned, it was the old gentleman who had the last laugh. While Mary was awaiting her trial she was told that her father's estate amounted to less than £4,000. The fortune of £10,000 – which had attracted Cranstoun – had either never existed, or been long spent. This was almost certainly the reason that Frances Blandy had set his face against so many aspiring suitors – because he was unable to provide the promised dowry. The irony of the situation must have come home to him on his deathbed; he had wronged his daughter by witholding the truth, and now she had poisoned him to obtain a non-existent fortune. This would seem to explain why he asked the weeping girl: "How canst thou think I could curse thee?"; after all, he had only himself to blame.

It was not until the end of the eighteenth century that poison ceased to be the favourite weapon of the domestic murderer. This was because a number of scientists – notably Karl Scheele, Samuel Hahnemann and Johann Metzger – had devised methods of testing for the most popular of all poisons, arsenic. In 1809, a German poisoner named Anna Zwanziger was trapped when one of her victims was exhumed and found to be full of arsenic. Anna had been killing off the wives and fiancées of her male employers in the hope of supplanting them; she was executed by the sword in 1811.

The Praslin Case

Other scientific developments were also helping to bring killers to justice. In 1847, it was the remarkable new invention called the microscope that provided the solution of the most sensational *crime passionel* of the decade.

Charles-Louis Theobald, the Duc de Choiseul-Praslin, married his wife Fanny — a daughter of one of Napoleon's generals — in 1824, when she was sixteen and he nineteen. She was a woman of fiery temperament, with lesbian inclinations, and by the time she was thirty-four, and had borne nine children, she was corpulent and wrinkled. The duke, an introverted, withdrawn man, found her dominant ways intolerable, and ceased to frequent her bed. Yet there can be no doubt that the duchess continued to love her husband. Matters became increasingly strained when an attractive girl named Henriette Deluzy was engaged as the children's governess, and it soon became clear that the duke was strongly attracted to her. Whether she became his mistress is not known, but it seems certain that the duchess thought the worst. She told her husband to dismiss the girl; he replied that if Henriette left, he would go too. The duchess wrote him a number of pathetic letters, which make it clear that this was not the first time the duke had shown interest in other women, and that in spite of this, she still loved him.

Finally, the duchess got her way; Henriette Deluzy was dismissed — without even a reference. The duke continued to call on her, and the affair became the talk of Paris society. In June 1847, the duchess announced that she intended to seek a divorce, on the grounds of her husband's adultery with the governess. The duke was mad with fury; he would lose his children and his position at one blow. On the evening of 17 August, he went to see Henriette Deluzy, and returned home in the early hours of the morning. As dawn was breaking, the servants were electrified by a piercing scream. Then the bell connected to the duchess's bedroom began to ring. There was another scream. It looked as if burglars had broken in. The duke's valet and the duchess's maid crept to her door, and heard the crash of something falling over. They knocked and called, but there was no reply. They tried another door, but it had been wedged. A number of servants rushed to the garden, and looked up at the bedroom window; as they did so, the shutter opened, and several of them saw a man they recognized as the duke. It seemed that he had also heard the burglars and had entered his wife's bedroom. The servants rushed back indoors to help him fight the intruders. To their surprise, the bedroom door was now open. The room was in chaos, with overturned furniture, and splashes of blood on the walls. The duchess was sitting on the floor, half-propped against her bed; she was obviously dead. Her throat had been slashed, and her face bruised and battered.

As they were examining her, the duke walked into the room, and gave a scream as he saw his dead wife. "Some monster has murdered my beloved Fanny! Fetch a doctor." He claimed that he had only just been awakened by the noise.

Two passing gendarmes noticed that the front door was open, and came in to investigate. Soon the house in the Rue Faubourg-St-Honoré was full of policemen, including M. Allard, Vidocq's successor as head of the Sûreté. It took him very little time to dismiss the theory about burglars – to begin with, the duchess's jewels were untouched. Under the sofa, he found a Corsican pistol, covered with blood.

"Does anyone know whom this belongs to?", asked Allard.

To his surprise, the duke answered: "Yes, to me."

To this Allard asked: "But how did it get here?"

The duke's story was that he had heard cries for help, and rushed into his wife's bedroom, brandishing his pistol. Seeing that she was covered in blood, he had dropped the pistol to raise her up. As a result, he had become covered in blood. Seeing that his wife was dead, he went back to his bedroom to wash off the blood . . .

It was just plausible – except, of course, that he had told the servants that he had only just awakened. Allard went to the duke's bedroom, and pointed out that bloodstains led to

A plan of the Duchess de Praslin's bedchamber.

his door. The duke replied that he had been dripping with his wife's blood as he had returned. But the state of the duke's bedroom left little doubt of his guilt; there was a bloodstained handkerchief, the bloodstained hilt of a dagger, and a piece of bloodstained cord. And when the severed end of the bell-pull from the duchess's bedroom was found under her husband's shirt, Allard told the duke he was under arrest.

But suppose his story were true? Or suppose, at any rate, that he continued to insist that it was true? Was there any point at which his account could be positively disproved? He could claim that the servants had misunderstood him when they thought he said he had only just been awakened by the noise. He could claim that the shock of discovering his wife's dead body had led him to act in a strange and confused manner, carrying off the bloodstained cord and the bell-pull. A court might disbelieve him, yet still have difficulty proving that he murdered his wife.

The bloodstained pistol was turned over to the eminent pathologist Ambroise Tardieu, who had written the first treatise on hanging, proved the guilt of Dr de la Pomerais, and discovered "Tardieu spots", the spots of blood that form under the heart of people who have been suffocated. What the police wanted to know was whether the pistol had been dropped in the duchess's blood, or used as a weapon to batter her to death. With characteristic thoroughness, Tardieu studied the pistol, first under a magnifying glass, then a microscope. The first thing he discovered was a chestnut hair close to the butt. Near the trigger guard, he found fragments of skin tissue. Further microscopic examination revealed a bulb, or root, of human hair, and more fragments of flesh. One of the fragments melted when heated, and formed a grease spot on a piece of paper. Moreover, some of the contused wounds on the dead woman's forehead had been made with a blunt instrument like the butt of the pistol. In short, there could be no possible doubt. The microscope revealed that the duchess had been battered to death with the pistol.

Tardieu's medical investigations revealed exactly what had happened that night. The Duc de Praslin had slipped into his wife's bedroom, probably through the bathroom, intending to kill her with one sweep of a sharp knife. But his nerve failed him, or perhaps she woke up as he bent over her. The blade made a deep cut in her throat, but failed to sever the windpipe; she screamed, and began to fight. He stabbed her again and again with a dagger, then began to beat her with the butt of the pistol; as she writhed on the floor, she bit his leg (a medical examination revealed her teeth marks). By this time the whole house was aroused; the servants were knocking on the door. His original plan – of killing her, then opening the front door and making it look like a burglary – had to be abandoned; instead, he decided to leave an open window. But as he threw back the shutters, he saw the servants in the garden. At least this allowed him to escape back to his own bedroom. And now he made yet another mistake. He rushed into his wife's room, pretending that the noise had awakened him, and screamed at the sight of his wife's body. And when the police arrived, and he was forced to change his story, he knew that his last chance of getting away with murder had vanished . . .

Before being taken off to the Luxembourg prison, the duke succeeded in swallowing a dose of arsenic. He died three days later, still refusing to admit to the murder. But Tardieu's microscope had made such a confession superfluous.

Madeleine Smith

In Glasgow in 1855, an attractive but bored nineteen-year-old girl named Madeleine Smith, daughter of a well-to-do architect, was introduced in the street to Pierre L'Angelier, a young Frenchman from Jersey, who had gone to considerable trouble to engineer the introduction. Soon afterwards, Madeleine received a letter from L'Angelier declaring his love; she replied encouragingly, using the maid as a go-between. The course of true love was far from smooth; when her parents found out, they ordered her never to communicate with him again. But the lovers continued to snatch brief and frustrating meetings, during which they exchanged hasty kisses and caresses. By December she was addressing him as "My own darling husband". But no real intimacy was possible between them until the following summer, when the Smiths went to their country house at

Row; here Madeleine had a chance to take unchaperoned country walks. A letter to L'Angelier in June 1856 begins: "If we did wrong last night, it was in the excitement of our love", and went on to note prosaically: "I did not bleed in the least but I had a good deal of pain during the night."

But later that summer, disillusionment — or perhaps merely satiety — began to set in. This may have had something to do with the attentions of a wealthy bachelor named William Minnoch, a close friend of her father's, who eventually proposed. Madeleine accepted. And at this point, L'Angelier played into her hands with a fit of petulance that led him to return one of her letters; she promptly replied that their engagement was at an end. "My love for you has ceased." L'Angelier's response was to threaten to write to her father revealing all. Madeleine hastily agreed to meet him again; again her letters address him as "dearest pet" and "sweet love"; but no longer as "My darling husband". For the truth was that she loathed the ungentlemanly blackmailer with her whole heart. They had two more meetings, each in the basement of Madeleine's house, and on each occasion he drank a cup of cocoa prepared by Madeleine. After the first meeting, L'Angelier was ill; after the second, in March 1857, he returned home in agony, bent over and clutching his stomach; by 11 o'clock the next morning he was dead. His doctor insisted on a post-mortem, and eighty-seven grains of arsenic were found in his stomach — the lethal dose being three grains.

Madeleine's letters were found; she immediately became the chief suspect, and was arrested on 31 March. The notion of a young girl becoming the mistress of a Frenchman horrified Scottish public opinion. Her guilt seemed obvious. Yet although it was proved that she had purchased three lots of arsenic, as rat poison, they had been mixed with soot or indigo. And no signs of soot or indigo were found in the dead man's stomach — but one medical witness commented that the grains of indigo could easily be washed from the

When London typist Elsie Cameron called on her lover Norman Thorne at his chicken farm at Crowborough, Sussex, to announce her pregnancy, she disappeared from sight. Her father telegraphed to ask her whereabouts; Thorne telegraphed back: "Not here . . . can't understand". Questioned by police and press, he insisted that he had not seen her.

When, a month later, a female neighbour reported that she had seen Elsie Cameron walking through the gate of the chicken farm on the day of her disappearance, police began digging. They found her dismembered body in a chicken run – buried in the exact spot at which Thorne had been photographed by a newspaper, feeding the chickens.

Thorne now claimed that he had stormed out of the hut after a quarrel with Elsie, and found her hanging from a beam when he returned.

Police pathologist Sir Bernard Spilsbury pointed out injuries to her face and head indicating heavy blows. Thorne's credibility was further dented by the discovery that there was no rope mark on the beam – on the contrary, the dust on top of the beam was undisturbed. If Thorne had pleaded manslaughter, he would probably have escaped with a prison sentence; as it was, his insistence on the suicide story led inevitably to a guilty verdict. He was hanged in April 1925.

In fact, Elsie had been bluffing; she was not pregnant.

Madelaine Smith in court.

arsenic with cold water. Madeleine insisted that her lover was in a habit of taking small quantities of arsenic for health reasons (arsenic is a stimulant and improves the complexion), but the defence offered no proof of this assertion. The jury eventually brought in a verdict of "not proven" — peculiar to Scotland — which implied that they regarded her as guilty, but found the proof insufficient. The crowd in court cheered, evidently feeling that L'Angelier deserved what he got.

Madeleine did not marry William Minnoch. Instead, she went to London, where she married a man named Hora, and became a successful hostess. The artist George du Maurier is said to have attended a Hora soirée and, unaware of the identity of his hostess, remarked "Madeleine Smith's beauty shouldn't have saved her from the scaffold." She later married an artist, George Wardle, who became manager of William Morris's silk weaving firm, and she developed an interest in socialism; Bernard Shaw once ate at her table. She died in America at the age of ninety-two.

Chapter Three

The Eternal
Triangle

M ost famous crimes of passion involve an "eternal triangle"
— husband, wife and lover (or mistress) — and in the
majority of these, the murderer and the lover are partners in
crime. But there is another type of eternal triangle in which the
lover — or mistress — remains innocent, a mere catalyst who
happens to inspire the crime. The most celebrated example of the
"catalyst" effect occurred in the Crippen case, which we shall
examine in the next chapter. But an earlier case, that of Dr Cross,
provides an equally interesting example.

Dr Cross and the Catalyst Effect

A retired army surgeon, sixty-two years of age, Dr
Philip Cross lived comfortably with his wife and six
children at Shandy Hall, near Dripsey, County Cork. His
wife was twenty-two years his junior; they had been
married eighteen years, and it had been, on the whole, a
satisfactory marriage. In October 1886, Mrs Laura Cross
engaged a new governess for the children, a twenty-year-
old girl named Effie Skinner. Effie, like Ethel Le Neve, was
the catalyst type: not particularly pretty, but with something soft and yielding about her. As soon as he saw her,
the military, rather forbidding Dr Cross felt like a hawk
eyeing a sparrow. For the first time, he realized that his

marriage had been merely satisfactory, never ecstatic. It had never provided him with any real outlet for his male dominance.

One day, as Effie stood talking to him about the children, he bent and kissed her. He was afraid she would tell his wife or leave immediately. But she stayed, and his desire to possess her increased. His wife noticed it, and she took what seemed to her the sensible course: she sacked Effie. The girl was shattered, she went to Dublin, and when Dr Cross visited her there, she finally gave herself to him. Possession did not cool his desire; he wanted to be married to her, living in comfort in Shandy Hall.

Early in May, 1887, Mrs Cross began to suffer attacks of vomiting. Her husband told her she had a weak heart. She died on 1 June, and was buried three days later. Less than two weeks after this, he married Effie Skinner in London. At first, he decided that they had better keep the marriage a secret and live separately, but when he got back to Dripsey, he discovered the news had preceded him.

There seemed no point keeping Effie in London, so he moved her to Shandy Hall. Inevitably, there was gossip, and the police finally decided to act. Laura Cross was exhumed, and the coroner found 3.2 grains of arsenic in her body, as well as strychnine. There was no trace of heart disease.

The police were also able to trace the firm from whom Dr Cross had bought arsenic "for sheep dipping". Tried at the Munster Assizes in Cork, he was found guilty on 18 December, 1887, and hanged in the following January. Effie was so shocked by the realization that she had been the cause of the murder that she refused to see him in the condemned cell, and Cross's hair turned white overnight.

The classic murder case on which Theodore Dreiser based his famous novel *An American Tragedy* took place on 11 July, 1906. Chester Gillette, a twenty-two-year-old labourer with aspirations to rise in the world, worked in his uncle's skirt factory in Courtland, New York. There he had an affair with eighteen-year-old secretary Billie Brown and made her pregnant. By this time, Gillette had met an attractive young socialite at a dance and become engaged to her. When Billie threatened to disclose her condition to his uncle, Chester invited her out for a day's boating on Big Moose Lake. Later that day, he was seen walking in the woods, his clothes dripping wet. Checking into another hotel he asked the clerk "Has there been a drowning reported?" The clerk said no.

Billie's body, her face battered, came to the surface the following day, and an inquest found that she had been murdered. Gillette's replies to police questions were evasive. Charged with murder, his defence was that Billie had committed suicide. But he then changed his story and claimed that the boat had capsized accidentally. The tennis racket with which he had beaten her was found buried near the lake, and proved crucial in contributing to the guilty verdict. Gillette was electrocuted in March 1908. Seventeen years later, he was immortalized by Theodore Dreiser, whose *American Tragedy* became a best-seller.

Adelaide Bartlett

At the time Dr Cross was engaged in seducing Effie Skinner, another celebrated crime of passion was exciting the usual fever of morbid interest among British newspaper readers – in fact, moreso than usual, since the third member of the triangle was a clergyman who showed a regrettable lack of chivalry towards the woman with whom he may or may not have committed adultery.

Theodore Edwin Bartlett was a hard-working and highly ambitious grocer. By the time he was twenty-nine, he and his business partner owned a chain of small shops in south London. This explains why, although he was a good-looking man, fond of the open air, he had never married; life was too busy for romance. Then, one day in the early 1870s, he went to call on his brother Charles, who lived in Kingston, and was introduced to a dazzlingly attractive eighteen-year-old girl named Adelaide Blanche de la Tremoile. She had dark curly hair, large appealing eyes, and a sensual mouth. Edwin found her fascinating. But it seems likely that, at this stage, marriage did not enter his head. Adelaide was definitely a "lady", and therefore far above him socially. Then he learned that there was some odd secret in her background. Adelaide's mother had borne her out of wedlock. Her father was a wealthy Englishman who preferred to keep his identity secret – it has been suggested that he was a member of Queen Victoria's entourage when she visited France in 1855, and was therefore probably titled. Now Adelaide lived with a guardian in a house in Richmond – she was staying in the Kingston house as a guest of Charles's sixteen-year-old daughter. So it seemed that, although she was a "lady", her chances of being accepted into English society were minimal. Edwin saw his chance, and pursued it with single-minded vigour. He called on her when she returned to Richmond, and seems to have persuaded her guardian, or her father, that a virtuous and successful grocer would make a desirable husband. To Adelaide he explained solemnly that his intentions were more than pure — there was no element of carnal desire in his feeling for her, and when they were married, their relationship would be wholly platonic. And by way of proving his good faith, Edwin Bartlett packed off his newly-wedded bride to a ladies' finishing school in Stoke Newington. She came to stay with her husband during the school holidays but, according to Adelaide, their relationship was like that of father and daughter. And when she had finished at the Stoke New-ington school, Edwin sent her off to a convent in Brussels. She stayed there until 1877, two years after their marriage, when she returned home to a newly furnished flat above Edwin's largest shop in Herne Hill. And for just one month, life was pleasant and peaceful, and Adelaide no doubt enjoyed being a young married woman in charge of her first home. Then Edwin's mother died, and the dutiful son invited his father to come and live with them.

It was a mistake. The old man was a bad-tempered old sponger, and he had never liked Adelaide. He made himself so unpleasant that Adelaide ran away from home — there is evidence that she went to stay in the house in Kingston where Edwin had first met her. And this seems to have led to further trouble. Edwin's younger brother Frederick also lived in the house, and the old man suspected a love affair. One writer on the case states that she became Frederick's mistress, but there is no evidence whatsoever for this assertion. All we know is that the old man accused Adelaide of having an affair with Frederick, and that Edwin was so incensed that he made his father sign an apology, which was drawn up by a solicitor. Then an uneasy peace reigned in the household.

Four years later, in 1881, two things broke the monotony of their lower middle class lives: Edwin had a nervous breakdown (brought on, according to his father, by laying a

Adelaide Bartlett.

floor), and Adelaide had a stillborn baby. The latter accident was Edwin's fault; the nurse he engaged to look after his wife had sensed that this might be a difficult birth, and begged Edwin to call in a doctor. But the Victorian Edwin was rather shocked at the idea of another man "interfering with her", and refused. By the time a doctor was finally called in, the baby was dead.

Soon after this, perhaps to distract her, they moved to the village of Merton, near Wimbledon. Edwin's motive may also have been to get rid of his father – he selected a house that had no spare bedroom. So the old man was forced to find a home elsewhere.

Early in 1885 – the Bartletts had now been married ten years – the couple decided to try another place of worship one Sunday morning. They attended the Wesleyan chapel in Merton. The preacher that day was a young man named George Dyson. He had a black moustache, a receding hairline, and was of slight build. Dyson made a pastoral call soon after that. And when he told Edwin Bartlett that he was about to go to Trinity College, Dublin, to take his degree, Bartlett was deeply impressed. He had an almost pathetic admiration for anyone with education – he himself was an avid but disorganized reader. He cross-questioned Dyson about his studies, and pressed the young man to come and visit them again as soon as he returned from Dublin. Slightly overwhelmed – for he was modest and not very clever – Dyson agreed. And a warm, if rather peculiar friendship, began between these three rather lonely people.

Dyson found Edwin Bartlett "exceedingly odd". He seemed to have eccentric ideas on all kinds of subjects. For example, he was a devotee of a work called *Esoteric Anthropology* by Thomas Low Nichols, whose long sub-title declared it to be a "confidential" treatise on the passionate attractions and perversions of the most intimate relations between men and women. It was not, as the judge later assumed, disguised pornography, but an early "women's lib" discourse on the unfairness of using women as sexual objects. It recommended birth control, and suggested that sexual intercourse should only be practised for the purpose of begetting children. Another of Edwin's rather peculiar beliefs was that men should have two wives, one for "use" and one for intellectual companionship. He was also, like many Victorians, interested in hypnotism, and in the doctrines of Anton Mesmer, according to which human beings possess a "vital magnetic fluid" that can be passed from one to another.

Soon, Edwin Bartlett was professing the warmest affection for the Reverend Dyson. In fact, he proposed that Dyson should continue Adelaide's education, teaching her geography, history, Latin and mathematics. Dyson, who was making a mere hundred pounds a year, agreed. He would arrive in the morning while Edwin was out at business, and often stay all day. During most of this time, he was alone with Adelaide. Whether she became his mistress depends on one's final view of her guilt or innocence, but certainly she often sat at his feet, with her head on his knee, and he often kissed her, alone and in her husband's presence. And, oddly enough, Edwin seemed delighted with the whole arrangement. His wife was lonely — she had only one close female friend, a Mrs Alice Matthews — and now he had found her a male friend and teacher who could be trusted implicitly. Edwin had unlimited faith in clergymen. If he found Edwin still in the house when he came in for supper, he warmly pressed him to stay for the evening. When the Bartletts went to Dover for a month, Edwin tried to persuade Dyson to come too, and offered him a first class season ticket so he could rush down every time he was free. Dyson refused, but Edwin still found time to travel to Putney (where Dyson lived) and whisk him off to Dover as an overnight guest. And he asked Dyson to be an executor of his will, in which, naturally, he left everything to Adelaide.

Crimes of Passion

That September, the Bartletts moved into a new lodging — it was to be their last — in Victoria. Edwin told their new landlady, Mrs Doggett, that they would be having a regular visitor, a clergyman, as a dinner guest. And George Dyson continued to call as regularly as ever, travelling from Putney, where he was now in charge of his own church, on a season ticket presented by Edwin Bartlett. They even kept a special jacket and slippers for him to change into. Dyson was finding this close friendship with a young married woman disturbing, and he confessed openly to Edwin that he was growing attracted to Adelaide and that it was upsetting his work; he felt he ought to stop seeing them. Edwin dismissed the idea, assuring Dyson that Adelaide had become a better and nobler woman since she had known him. He seemed to be trying to throw them into one another's arms. And Mrs Doggett noticed one day, after Dyson had left, that the window curtains were not merely drawn, but pinned together. It is hard to imagine why they should do this unless, at the very least, they had been engaging in some heavy petting.

And now, suddenly, Edwin became ill. One day he felt so exhausted at work that he hurried home. The next morning, he and Adelaide and Dyson went to a dog show — dogs were one of Edwin's main interests — but he felt so ill that they had to return home. Adelaide went out to fetch a doctor. She found a young man called Alfred Leach, whom she had never met before, but who immediately accompanied her back home. Edwin was suffering from sickness, diarrhoea and bleeding of the bowels; he had also had toothache. When Dr Leach looked into his mouth, he observed a blue line round the gums, a symptom of mercury poisoning. When he asked Edwin if he had taken mercury, Edwin denied it, but admitted that he had swallowed a pill he had found in a drawer — he had no idea what it was for. Leach arrived at another explanation. Edwin's teeth were in an appalling condition and his breath smelt foul. Apparently the dentist who made his false teeth had failed to draw the stumps; for some reason, he had sawed off the teeth at the gums. When these had rotted, the dentist merely made more false teeth, and the condition of his mouth made it impossible for Edwin to clean his remaining teeth. Leach's theory was that Edwin had, at some time, got a dose of mercury into his system, and that the sulphides produced by his rotting teeth had combined with it to form mercuric sulphide, hence the blue line. A dentist who was called in verified that Edwin was suffering from mercury poisoning, and extracted fifteen roots and stumps.

So throughout December the patient remained in bed. On Christmas Day, 1885, he received an unpleasant shock when he went to the lavatory and passed a round worm. He was naturally something of a hypochondriac, and this gave him "the horrors". He swore that he could feel worms wriggling in his throat, and became deeply depressed.

On the last day of December, and the last day of Edwin's life, he went to the dentist for yet another tooth extraction. Young Dr Leach, who had become a devotee of Adelaide, went with them. On the way, Adelaide remarked that they had just been saying that they sometimes wished they were unmarried, so they could have the pleasure of getting married again. Later, when Edwin got home, his appetite had improved, and he ate a large meal of oysters, jugged hare and cake, with a helping of chutney. He told Mrs Doggett that he would have a haddock for his breakfast, Obviously, he was at last on the road to recovery.

Just before 4 a.m. on New Year's Day, Adelaide knocked on the Doggett's bedroom door. "Go and fetch Dr Leach. I think Mr Bartlett is dead." She explained that she had fallen asleep, holding Edwin's foot, which apparently soothed him, as she sat beside his bed. She had awakened and felt that he was cold. She had tried to revive him with brandy, but without success. Dr Leach observed a glass of brandy on the shelf, with a smell of chloroform.

The moment old Mr Bartlett heard of his son's death, he concluded he had been murdered. He sniffed his son's lips, then turned to Dr Leach and said, "We must have a post mortem."

The post mortem revealed a baffling and astonishing fact: that Edwin Bartlett had died of chloroform poisoning. This was so astonishing because chloroform is an unpleasant-tasting substance that would be almost impossible to swallow; moreover, it causes vomiting. If chloroform was poured down someone's throat when he was unconscious, for example, from the fumes of chloroform, it would get into the lungs. And there was no chloroform in Edwin Bartlett's lungs. Which seemed to point to the completely mystifying conclusion that Edwin Bartlett had drunk the chloroform voluntarily. Yet his cheerfulness before he went to sleep, and the fact that he had even ordered his breakfast, made it unlikely that he intended suicide.

And where had the chloroform come from? This was soon revealed. The Reverend Dyson had bought it, at Adelaide's request. He had even gone to three separate chemists to get a fairly large quantity, claiming that he wanted to use it as cleaning fluid. Adelaide had told him she wanted it to make her husband sleep. And now, when he heard that chloroform had been found in Edwin's stomach, Dyson was panic stricken. He saw it as the end of his career. He rushed along to see Adelaide, and when Mrs Matthews came unexpectedly into the room, she heard Dyston saying: "You did tell me Edwin was going to die soon." And when Adelaide denied it, he bowed his head on the piano and groaned: "Oh, my God!" Later that day, he saw Adelaide alone, and she asked him to say nothing about the chloroform. Dyson refused, and said he was going to make a clean breast of it.

And so he did. And the result was that Adelaide Bartlett found herself on trial for murder. When, in the spring of

1886, it became known that she was to be tried for poisoning her husband, and that the Reverend George Dyson would probably stand in the dock beside her, public excitement was intense. It had all the signs of being a thoroughly scandalous murder case, complete with revelations of secret adultery and a plot by the lovers to kill the husband. And when it was known that the great advocate Edward Clarke would defend Adelaide, people nodded significantly. Clarke was not one of those barristers who depended on verbal fireworks and bullying to win his cases; he was known for a certain quiet sincerity. Yet for all that, he had a formidable reputation. It was obvious that no suburban grocer's wife could afford his services, which could only mean that her mysterious father had intervened.

In the event, Adelaide finally stood alone in the dock; Dyson had managed to clear his own name by shamelessly doing his best to hand her over to the hangman. Edward Clarke had an apparently impossible task: to convince a Victorian jury that this pretty Frenchwoman, quite probably an adulteress, was innocent of her husband's murder. He had only one thing on his side: the total mystery of how even the most cunning murderess could have got the chloroform into Edwin Bartlett's stomach.

Clarke's defence was brilliant. His line of argument was that Edwin was a highly eccentric man who had almost thrown his wife into the arms of the clergyman, and who had actually told them that he expected them to get married when he was dead. He had insisted that his marriage to Adelaide should be purely platonic, and they had only had sexual intercourse once, as a result of which a baby had been born. But in the last days of his illness, Edwin had suddenly shown a desire for sexual intercourse. Adelaide felt this was wrong, since she now regarded herself as affianced to Dyson. So she asked Dyson to get her chloroform, so she might wave it in his face if he made sexual demands. However, she had been unable to go

The Pimlico poisoning case.

through with it. She had never been able to keep a secret from Edwin, and on that last evening of his life, had confessed her intention and showed him the bottle of chloroform. Edwin had been rather sulky about it, and had placed the bottle on the mantelpiece. And somehow, while Adelaide dozed by his side, holding his foot to comfort him, some of that chloroform had got into Edwin's stomach. (She admitted she had disposed of the rest by throwing it from the window of a train.) The main point of the defence was that Edwin was eccentric to the point of insanity, and that such an unpredictable man might easily have swallowed chloroform, perhaps simply to upset his wife and gain attention.

Amazingly enough, the jury swallowed this unlikely story of a wife too virtuous even to permit her own husband sexual intercourse, even when it was revealed that Edwin had rubber contraceptives in his pocket and undoubtedly used them in making love to Adelaide. But the central point of the defence, of course, was that baffling mystery of the chloroform: if Adelaide poisoned her husband, how did she get it into his stomach? To that question the prosecution had no answer. After that, there could only be one verdict. "Although we think there is the gravest suspicion attaching to the prisoner, we do not think there is sufficient evidence to show how or by whom the chloroform was administered." So the verdict had to be not guilty. The judge had to reprove the court sternly as it burst into cheers.

The question of Adelaide's guilt or innocence has been argued by criminologists ever since. Some, like Nigel Morland, have no doubt that she was innocent, and that Edwin took the chloroform himself in a spirit of resentment or mischief. The majority are inclined to believe that Adelaide was poisoning Edwin from the beginning with some mercury compound, and only decided on the dangerous expedient of ether when he looked like recovering. And one, Yseult Bridges, believes that Adelaide somehow used hypnosis to induce Edwin to swallow the chloroform. None, as far as I know, have hit upon what seems to be the simplest and most obvious solution.

Let us try to reconstruct a hypothetical scenario. When Edwin Bartlett meets the beautiful Adelaide, he is too shy to hope that she will become his mistress as well as his wife, and so he assures her that their relationship will be a purely platonic one. But after two years of marriage, he is less humble and self-effacing, and insists on his marital rights. As a result, Adelaide becomes pregnant, but due to her husband's peculiar ideas about doctors, she loses the baby.

Edwin's curious attitude, his feeling that a doctor who examined his wife would be "interfering with her", indicates a powerful physical jealousy. It is surely the attitude of a man who has the utmost difficulty in persuading his wife to permit him the use of her body, so the idea of another man examining her intimately arouses intense jealousy. Adelaide, for her part, finds sex with her husband rather unpleasant, perhaps because his rotten teeth cause permanent halitosis, and she does her best to persuade him to abide by their "platonic" contract by petting him, fussing over him, showing him a great deal of affection, in fact, everything but allowing him into her bed. (At the trial, it was emphasized that they seemed to be an extremely happily married couple.) She makes use of the standard excuse, that she is afraid of becoming pregnant again, but Edwin counters that by buying contraceptives.

For Edwin, life becomes a permanent siege on his wife's virtue, with very infrequent successes. In his efforts to soften her, he deliberately introduces the Reverend George Dyson into their household, and encourages a flirtation. In effect, he is asking the clergyman, whom he trusts implicitly, to "warm her up". While she is feeling kindly and grateful to her husband, she can hardly refuse him the occasional embrace.

Edwin falls ill; we do not know whether, as Yseult Bridges believes, she has been administering small doses of lead acetate or some mercuric poison. But it gives her a flash of hope, she sees the end of her martyrdom in sight. Then he begins to recover and to indicate that his sexual appetites are returning to normal. Perhaps she finds the contraceptives in his pocket.

And it is at this point that she asks Dyson to buy the chloroform. Presumably the idea of killing Edwin is at the back of her mind — it is hard to believe that she intends to soak a hankerchief in the drug and try and press it over his nose whenever he becomes amorous. But she also knows Edwin well enough to know that, as a hypochondriacal invalid, he quite enjoys taking "medicines". He is in a state of neurotic depression about his "worms". Dr Leach has given him all kinds of medicines for them, without effect — Edwin is convinced he is still swarming with worms. All Adelaide needs to do is to produce the chloroform, and tell Edwin that Dr Leach has recommended this to get rid of worms. Perhaps only the lightest of hints is needed. Perhaps she offers him a little chloroform mixed with brandy, but he finds it unpleasant. Then, as she sits beside him, holding his foot and breathing deeply, he decides that he will win her approval by taking his medicine, and he cautiously reaches out for the bottle.

Sir James Paget, a well-known doctor, made the famous comment: "Now the case is over, she should tell us in the interests of science how she did it". The answer is surely that she did not do it, Edwin did. Whether it was at Adelaide's suggestion we shall never know.

Mrs Maybrick

Because she was suspected of adultery, Adelaide Bartlett was fortunate to avoid meeting the hangman. Because she undoubtedly *had* committed adultery, her younger contemporary Florence Maybrick came an uncomfortable shade closer to the gallows. Both women were married to drug-taking hypochondriacs, but Mrs Maybrick's defence failed to convince the judge or jury at her trial for murder.

Florence Chandler, born in Mobile, Alabama in 1862, was a "southern belle" in the tradition of Scarlett O'Hara; her father was a wealthy banker, and her main aim in life was to secure a rich husband. He appeared on the scene when she was eighteen – an overweight, forty-one-year-old English cotton broker named James Maybrick, whom she met on a ship crossing the Atlantic. When she accepted his proposal, Florence may have suspected that he was not a virgin, but she was certainly unaware that he had an

The great American *cause célèbre* of 1904 was the trial of *Floradora* girl Nan Patterson for the murder of her lover Caesar Young in a hansom cab. The shot that killed gambler Caesar Young was fired at about 8 o'clock on the morning of 4 June, 1904; he was dead by the time he reached hospital. Nan Patterson claimed he committed suicide but the police disbelieved her – to begin with, the revolver was in Young's pocket, and it seemed unlikely he would have placed it there after shooting himself.

Young, who was married, had met Nan Patterson on a train to California two years earlier. It was a passionate affair, but by 1904, Young wanted to terminate it; to that end he booked passage for Europe for himself and his wife on the *Germanic*. He and Nan spent a last evening quarrelling violently. He nevertheless met her for a breakfast of brandy and whiskey, after which they called the hansom, and Young was shot soon after. Under the circumstances, Nan's story that he killed himself because he was upset about leaving her seemed unlikely – the bullet had entered at the wrong angle. At her first trial, a juror became ill, so a mis-trial was declared. Her second trial ended with a hung jury. When the third trial also ended in deadlock, all charges against her were dropped. In retrospect it seems clear that Nan was acquitted, not because she was innocent, but because the men on the jury felt she was too pretty to hang.

Nan cashed in her notoriety by accepting leading roles in various musicals, but proved to lack talent, and soon vanished into obscurity.

American mistress named Mary Hogwood, by whom he had sired three children.

For a while the newlyweds lived in Norfolk, Virginia, where Maybrick spent his days at the cotton exchange. A male child was born there. When they moved back to Liverpool two years later, another child, this time a girl, arrived. It was soon after this that Florence learned that her husband had a mistress named Mary Hogwood, and that Mary had given birth to two more children since James Maybrick's marriage. She was upset, but accepted the "double standard" that was current in the late Victorian age. And for another four years, life continued uneventfully at Battlecrease House, their home in the Liverpool suburb of Aigburth.

The Maybricks often gave dinner parties, and it was at one of these in December 1888 that Florence met a tall, good-looking man named Alfred Brierley, a thirty-eight-year-old bachelor who was, like her husband, a successful cotton broker. She saw him a great many times that winter, and when the spring came, Brierley accompanied the Maybricks on a tour of the spring race meetings. Brierley's obvious admiration was welcome; her husband was frequently bad tempered, and had ceased to treat her with the courtliness a southern belle expected. Brierley, on the other hand, behaved like a medieval knight.

So when her husband went to London alone on 12 March, 1889, and Brierley took the opportunity to tell Florence he loved her, she admitted shyly that she returned the feeling. Brierley went on to press her to go away with him — but he was not thinking of an elopement, only of a dirty weekend. By this time, Florence was as eager to commit adultery as he was, and agreed.

It happened a week later. Telling her husband that she was going to stay with an aunt who was about to have an operation, Florence checked into a small hotel in London. Brierley took another suite. That night, Mrs Maybrick spent the night in Brierley's suite; the following night, he slept in hers. But although both suites had been reserved for a week, they checked out after only three days. This may have been because, having satisfied their curiosity, they were tired of one another, or possibly because Florence wished to establish an alibi. She went to stay with her cousin Margaret Baillie.

The day after she returned home, she and her husband attended the Grand National at Aintree. Brierley was also there, and he offered to take Florence to take a look at the Prince of Wales in the grandstand. By this time, Maybrick seems to have begun to develop belated suspicions; when his wife returned, he told her angrily that she had been away too long.

That evening, the Maybricks had a noisy quarrel, and he ordered her to leave the house, sending for a cab. In fact, the cab was finally dismissed, and Florence spent the night in a room next to the nursery. The next morning, she had a black eye. That day, Mrs Maybrick told a female confidant that she wanted a divorce. The family doctor intervened, and the Maybricks apparently made up their quarrel – even when Mrs Maybrick revealed that she was heavily in debt to money lenders. But harsh words were exchanged again the next day. After sounds of a noisy altercation, the servants found Florence in a faint. She spent a week in bed.

On 8 April, Florence went to see Alfred Brierley to display her black eye; she was evidently hoping that he would propose an elopement. Instead he looked embarrassed and got rid of her as soon as possible.

In mid-April, James Maybrick went to London to pay off another of his wife's creditors. He also took the opportunity to see a doctor about pains in the head and numbness in the limbs. The doctor prescribed various medicines for indigestion and constipation. He does not seem to have been aware that Maybrick made a habit of dosing himself with arsenic and strychnine, both of which are stimulants when taken in

Mrs James Maybrick.

small quantities, and which can produce the symptoms Maybrick complained about. He seems to have been concerned enough to re-draft his will — although he now left most of his estate to the children.

Soon after this, Florence bought no less than two dozen fly papers from the local chemist — the old fashioned type consisting of a sheet of paper soaked in a solution of arsenic. A servant noticed that the fly papers were soaking in water in a sink. A week later, Mrs Maybrick ordered yet another two dozen. Three days later, on 27 April, 1889, James Maybrick had a severe attack of vomiting. He attended the Wirral races, but his hand was so shaky that he spilt his wine when dining with friends.

As the attacks of indigestion continued on into May, the servants — who were inclined to be hostile to Florence — informed some of Maybrick's friends that they suspected his wife of poisoning him. Maybrick's brother Michael arrived from London, and ordered that no one but a nurse was to attend the sick man. When he caught Florence pouring medicine from one bottle to another, he shouted at her and took charge of the medicine, refusing to accept her explanation that it had so much sediment that a bigger bottle was more convenient for shaking. Michael took the medicine for analysis, but it proved to contain no poison. Neither did some food that Michael confiscated and took to the same doctor.

Nevertheless, on 11 May, James Maybrick died. A post mortem showed stomach inflammation due to "some irritant substance". On 14 May, Florence was arrested and charged with his murder.

One thing was quite clear: that Maybrick had been for years in the habit of taking various dangerous substances as stimulants, including arsenic and strychnine. In any modern court of law, this would have been sufficient to ensure his wife's acquittal. Moreover, even the Home Office expert, Dr Thomas Stevenson, admitted that

In France, the most sensational murder trial of
1890 was that of a pimp named Michel Eyraud
and his attractive but unscrupulous mistress
Gabrielle Bompard. She lured a wealthy
businessman named Gouffé to her room, where
Eyraud strangled him. The corpse was then
placed in a trunk and dumped in a wood near
Lyon. By the time the trunk was found, the
body was so decomposed as to be
unrecognisable. But brilliant forensic work by
the great pathologist Alexandre Lacassagne,
revealed a legbone malformation that proved
the body to be that of the missing Gouffé.
Eyraud fled to America, was recognised in Cuba
through a newspaper photograph, and was taken
back to Paris to face the guillotine; his mistress
received life imprisonment.

arsenic is a cumulative poison that will be stored up
in the system; this in itself should have been enough to
acquit Florence Maybrick.

Unfortunately, her three nights in London with Alfred
Brierley had become known. Three days before her husband's death, she had written him a letter describing her
husband as "sick unto death", and telling Brierley that there
was "no fear of discovery". A servant intercepted it and
handed it to Michael Maybrick. And although the letter
contained no evidence that Florence was poisoning her
husband, it virtually condemned her. Before a hostile jury,
and an audience that hissed her, Mrs Maybrick heard Mr
Justice Fitzjames Stephen read the sentence of death on
Wednesday 7 August, 1889. The date of execution was
fixed for 26 August.

Crimes of Passion

The verdict caused nationwide indignation. But in those days there was no court of appeal. Thousands of people signed a petition for mercy. Even Maybrick's ex-mistress, Mary Hogwood, wrote from Virginia to say that he took arsenic all the time, and that she had fully expected him to die of it. Three days before she was due to hang, Florence Maybrick's sentence was commuted to life imprisonment.

She was released in 1904, and returned to America, where she wrote a book called *My Fifteen Lost Years*, and became a popular lecturer, never failing to move her audience with her simple statement: "I swear to you I am innocent." She spent the later years of her life as a recluse, surrounded by cats, dying in 1939. Her son Jim, convinced that she had murdered his father, forbade her to see her daughter Gladys; he carried a photograph of his father with him to the day of his death. Oddly enough, he also died of poison. Working in a laboratory in British Columbia, Canada, in 1911, he accidentally picked up a beaker containing cyanide – instead of water – to wash down a sandwich, and died soon after.

America differed from England in never having had a "Victorian age". Nineteenth century America was noisy, vulgar and almost painfully alive. Mrs Fanny Trollope – mother of the novelist – and Charles Dickens took one look at the United States, and hurried back to England to write highly critical travel sketches. But American crudeness was counterbalanced by sheer inventiveness and an endless capacity for innovation. This was as apparent in its crimes of passion as in its railroads and dime stores. In 1895, a Sunday school teacher named Theodore Durrant lured two virtuous girls – separately – into the Baptist church on Bartlett Street in San Francisco, where he killed and raped them. The first, Blanche Lamont, was placed in the belfry; the second, Minnie Williams, was left in the library where she had been stabbed to death. Durrant had been seen with both girls just before they vanished, and was found guilty and sentenced to death. In the days when sex crime was virtually unknown, the Durrant case made headlines all round the world.

In 1897, a Chicago sausage maker named Adolph Luetgart, who had more than one mistress, decided to dispose of his wife in such a way that her body would never be found; he boiled her in one of his sausage vats, turning her into soft soap with a solution of caustic potash. He overlooked one small detail: his wife's rings. These were found in the bottom of the vat, together with a false tooth and a sesamoid bone from the human foot. Nevertheless, Luetgart's ingenuity was not entirely wasted, because he was convicted on purely medical evidence, he escaped the death penalty and was sentenced to life imprisonment.

The Guldensuppe Case

It was also in 1897 — on 26 June — that two teenagers who were swimming in the East River near the foot of 11th Street discovered a floating parcel that proved to contain human remains. The headless torso was wrapped in a red and gold oilcloth with a cabbage rose pattern, and the hairy chest had a patch of skin missing, suggesting that a tattoo had been removed; the mutilations seemed to indicate surgical skill. The next day, the lower half of the body, minus the legs, was found in woods near 176th Street — the legs were later found by another two boys swimming off the Brooklyn shore.

The newspaper magnate William Randolph Hearst, virtually the inventor of the "Yellow Press", saw an opportunity to sell more of his newspapers, and assigned a "murder squad" of reporters to the case. One of these, George Arnold, was inspecting the remains (now complete except for the head) in the city morgue when he observed that the hands and the fingers were heavily calloused. Arnold was a devotee of the Turkish baths, and he knew that masseurs develop the same kind of callouses. Since the big man on the slab looked vaguely familiar, he hurried down to his favourite establishment in Murray Hill and asked if any of the masseurs had failed to report for duty. The answer was that a man called Willie Guldensuppe had not been in for two days. And he had a tattoo on his chest. Guldensuppe had lived at a boarding-house at 439 Ninth Avenue, which was run by an unlicensed midwife called Augusta Nack.

Hearst's "murder squad" now set out to trace the distinctive oilcloth in which the remains had been wrapped, and the newspaper, the *Journal*, published appeals for information, and a coloured reproduction of the oilcloth. It was a Hearst reporter who was making a round of dry goods stores on Long Island who found the dealer who had sold the oilcloth; the man's name was Max Riger, and he described the woman who had purchased it as a well-built but not unattractive lady. Since this description fitted Augusta Nack — who had the dimensions of an opera singer — Hearst reporters galloped off to the Ninth Street boarding-house, narrowly forestalling those of a rival newspaper, the *World*, and persuaded Augusta Nack to accompany them to the police headquarters. To keep rival reporters away, Hearst rented the whole boarding-house and placed guards on the door; they even severed the telephone wires.

The police decided on shock tactics, and took Mrs Nack to view the remains. Pointing to the legs, the detective asked: "Are those Willie's?"

Mrs Nack looked at him haughtily. "I would not know, as I never saw the gentleman naked."

But the *Journal* reporters had heard another story from the inhabitants of the boarding-house and from neighbours. They asserted that Mrs Nack and Willie Guldensuppe had been lovers for years. But they had quarrelled recently, the cause apparently being a fellow lodger, a young barber named Martin Thorn.

The police managed to forestall the *Journal* reporters at the barber shop where Thorn worked. There another barber named John Gotha told them that Thorn had confessed the murder of Willie Guldensuppe to him. Thorn's story was that Mrs Nack had seduced him when her regular lover, Guldensuppe, was away. But when Guldensuppe had found them in bed together, the brawny masseur had beaten Thorn so badly that the barber had to go into hospital. And when he reported for work with two black eyes, he was dismissed. Thorn decided to change his lodgings. But Mrs Nack had continued to visit him there. And Thorn had purchased a stiletto and a pistol, determined to revenge himself . . .

Martin Thorn was arrested, and the *Journal* headline declared: MURDER MYSTERY SOLVED BY JOURNAL. By now, both the *Journal* and the police had located the spot where the murder took place. It was in a pleasantly rural area on Long Island called Woodside, not far from the store where the oilcloth had been purchased. A farm stood next to the cottage, and on the day Willie Guldensuppe's torso had been recovered from the river, the farmer had been puzzled to see that his ducks had turned a pink colour. The reason, he soon discovered, was that they had been bathing in a large pool of pink-coloured water, which had issued from the bathroom drainage pipe of the cottage next door. But it was not until the farmer read of the arrest of Martin Thorn and Augusta Nack that he connected this event with a couple who had rented the cottage two weeks earlier. They had called themselves Mr and Mrs Braun, and had paid $15 rent in advance. But they had only visited the cottage on two occasions, the second on the day of the disappearance of Willie Guldensuppe . . . Belatedly, the farmer decided to pass on his suspicions to the police.

Crimes of Passion

> In 1914, 138 articles and cartoons appeared in the Paris newspaper *Le Figaro* deriding the finance minister Joseph Caillaux. On 13 March, 1914, Mme Henriette Caillaux, his wife, strode into the office of *Le Figaro* and shot dead its leading columnist – and the man largely responsible for the lampoons – Gaston Calmette.
>
> Tried the following July, Mme Caillaux pleaded great provocation, and that the gun had gone off accidentally. She was acquitted.

A revolver, a carving knife and a saw were found in the cottage; but, advised by their respective lawyers, the two declined to confess. Thorn succeeded in escaping to Canada and was brought back; yet even when shown the "confession" he had allegedly made to John Gotha, he continued to insist on his total innocence.

The difference between the Nack-Thorn trial and that of Eyraud and Bompard is a measure of the difference between Paris and New York in the *fin de siècle* period; the French would have been horrified by the carelessness and levity of the American courtroom. Thorn was represented by a brilliant but not over-scrupulous lawyer named Howe, whose line of defence was simply that the two defendants were unacquainted with one another, and that neither of them knew the victim anyway. What evidence was there, asked Howe, that the assorted arms and legs belonged to Willie Goldensoup? (On other occasions he pronounced it Gludensop, Gildersleeve, Goldylocks and Silverslipper.) They might belong to any corpse. What evidence was there that the victim had ever existed?

This audacious line of defence might well have succeeded — New York jurors liked to be amused, and Howe had talked innumerable clients out of the electric chair — except that Mrs Nack decided to confess. Hearst had sent a Presbyterian minister to see her in prison every day, and one day he had brought his son, a curly-haired child of four, who climbed on to her lap and begged her to clear her conscience; Hearst naturally printed the story a day ahead of his rivals. And on the second day of the trial, Mrs Nack declared that she had seen the light, and gave a gruesomely detailed account of the crime. On the day before the murder, she and Martin Thorn had rented the cottage on Long Island. She then told Willie Guldensuppe that she had decided to run it as a baby farm, and asked him to come and give his opinion. When Willie entered the building, Thorn was waiting behind a door, and shot him in the back of the head. Then they threw him into the empty bathtub and, while he still breathed stertorously, Thorn sawed off his head. While Mrs Nack went out to buy oilcloth, Thorn dismembered the body — he had once been a medical student, which explained the surgical skill noticed by the police surgeon. He left the taps running, under the impression that the water would run down a drain and into the sewers; in fact, there was no drain, and it formed a pool in the farmyard, where the ducks were delighted at the opportunity of a midsummer bathe. Thorn then encased the head in plaster of Paris, and threw it in the river . . .

The narrative so upset one of the jurors that he fainted and had to be carried out of court. This caused a mis-trial, and when the case was resumed, Thorn had changed his story. He now declared that the cottage had been rented only as a love nest, and that on the day of the murder, he had arrived to find Mrs Nack already there. "Willie's upstairs. I've just killed him." Once again, Howe rested his defence upon the assertion that there was no proof that the corpse was that of Willie Guldensuppe, and for a while it looked as if the absence of an American Lacassagne might sway the issue in favour of the accused. But the jury chose to be convinced by the negative evidence of the missing tattoo, and found them both guilty. Martin Thorn went to the electric chair; Mrs Nack was sentenced to twenty years. The *Journal* was jubilant, but the *World* took the view that Thorn was the victim of a scheming woman.

Mrs Nack was apparently an exemplary prisoner, and was paroled after ten years; she returned to her old neighbourhood on Ninth Avenue and opened a delicatessen shop; but for some reason, the neighbours found her cooked meats unattractive, and she retired into obscurity.

Chapter Four

Sexual Deviants

I n 1902, Queen Victoria had been dead for only a year, and Britain was still governed by Victorian morality. This meant inevitably that any crime that involved an element of sex scandal aroused far more excitement than a crime that merely involved violence against the person. Which in turn explains the widespread press coverage given to "the Peasenhall mystery" — although in the age of the serial killer, its details seem commonplace enough.

The Peasenhall Mystery

1 June, 1902, was a bright, sunny morning after a night of storm. William Harsent, a carter, walked through the peaceful Suffolk village of Peasenhall, on his way to take clean linen to his daughter Rose. He walked through the wet garden of Providence House, where the girl was in service, and pushed open the back door. What he saw made him drop the linen. Rose Harsent lay, half naked, at the foot of the stairs. Her throat was cut from ear to ear, and deep gashes covered her bare shoulders. She had been wearing a nightdress, but this had been partly torn from her, and partly burnt away. A broken medicine bottle lay on the floor beside the body.

The local policeman arrived, followed by the doctor. The policeman discovered that the broken medicine bottle had contained paraffin — which had apparently been used in the attempt to burn her. The girl's bed had not been slept in, but

73

there were three letters in the room, one of which made an appointment to come and see her at midnight.

The signature made it clear that the author was William Gardiner, a young foreman carpenter who lived nearby; he had a wife and six children, and was known as a devout Methodist. Medical examination revealed that Rose Harsent had been dead at least four hours, and that she had been pregnant.

No one had any doubt that the father of the unborn child was William Gardiner, for in the previous year he and Rose had been the subject of scandal in Peasenhall. Two youths had seen them walking towards an empty cottage known as the "Doctor's Chapel", which stood alone in a field. The youths had hidden behind a hedge until the two had gone inside, then crept closer. They were unable to see what was happening, but the sounds made it clear. There was a rustling of clothes, then the girl gasped "Oh, oh."

The silence that followed seemed to suggest a state of mutual satisfaction. Gardiner was heard to ask her what she was thinking. She answered: "What you were reading last Sunday." He asked her what he had been reading, and she replied: "About what we are doing now." She then went on to quote the verses from Genesis, chapter 38, about how Onan "spilled his seed on the ground".

When the story was repeated in Peasenhall, the villagers, who knew their Bible, had no doubt that Gardiner and Rose Harsent had either been engaged in extremely intimate "petting", or that the youths had overheard an act of *coitus interruptus*. Gardiner was a Sunday School teacher; Rose Harsent was one of his choir girls.

The scandal was so great that an enquiry had been conducted by the Reverend John Grey; Gardiner had denied the story, saying that he had been in the "chapel" with the girl only to help her move a stiff door. Gardiner had been told "Let this be a warning to you for life", and had appeared to be suitably chastened. Yet although he promised to have nothing further to do with the girl, it was plain to people who observed them closely that they were still on intimate terms.

The day after Rose Harsent's body was found, a superintendent of police called on Gardiner, and asked him if the handwriting on one of the letters was his; Gardiner denied it. The policeman asked if the envelope in which a certain letter was contained was not identical with those used by Gardiner's building firm; again he denied it. But the next day, he was arrested and charged with Rose's murder.

Certainly, the case against him looked black. His clasp knife was found to be stained with blood, although he claimed he had been cutting up rabbits: in 1902, there was no way of testing whether a bloodstain was from a human being or an animal; Paul Uhlenhuth *had* discovered the basic principle in 1900, but it had never been used outside Germany.

Various witnesses said that they saw a large fire burning at the back of Gardiner's house on the morning after the murder; the prosecution argued that this explained why no bloodstained clothing was found in the house; Gardiner's wife testified that there had been a fire, but that it was only the usual fire they lit on Sundays; but she did not explain why they needed a fire on a hot June morning.

Gardiner's defence was an alibi, supported by his wife; he said he had been at home all evening, and been in bed beside his wife all night. Gardiner was lucky. In those days the jury's verdict in a murder trial had to be unanimous, and one member of the jury stubbornly refused to be convinced of his guilt. The judge had to order a retrial, and once again the jury failed to agree.

Gardiner should have been tried a third time; but the authorities decided he had been through enough, and entered a *nolle prosequi* – which meant no further prosecution would take place. It was equivalent to the Scottish verdict of "not proven". Gardiner and his wife moved to a

London suburb, where they opened a shop. Whether they prospered or not has never been recorded.

Was Gardiner guilty? We can never know. Certainly, Gardiner was not the only man who might have made Rose pregnant. Highly indecent verses were found in her room, and proved to have been written by the youth next door, who was in love with her. She was no blushing wallflower, but a forthright country girl who had no objection to keeping obscene verses. She may well have had other lovers beside Gardiner – a solution adopted by Brian Cooper in *Genesis 38* his novel about the murder, which suggests that the dissenting jury man who saved Gardiner's neck at the first trial knew the identity of the real murderer.

Only one thing is clear: Gardiner came close to the gallows, not because the evidence against him was particularly strong, but because the jury found it hard to forget that this Sunday School teacher had misbehaved himself on the floor of a disused cottage with one of his choir girls.

The Crippen Case

In the year 1908, a young medical assistant succeeded his superior, Dr Pepper, as pathologist at St Mary's Hospital, London. Bernard Spilsbury was recently married, and had been receiving a salary of only £200 a year. Two years later, Spilsbury achieved sudden fame as a result of the most sensational murder trial of the decade.

Dr Harvey Hawley Crippen was an American whose medical degrees, if they existed, would not have allowed him to practise in England; his diploma came from a college of homoeopathy, still regarded by many members of the medical profession as a crank aberration. He was a thirty-year-old widower when, in 1892, he met a nineteen-year-old Polish girl who had anglicized her name to Cora Turner.

Dr Crippen.

Crimes of Passion

She was the mistress of a stove manufacturer, who had set her up in a flat and was paying for her singing lessons — Cora was convinced she would become a great singer. The notion of being a doctor's wife appealed to her, and she induced Crippen to propose by telling him that her lover wanted her to run away with him. The great depression of 1893 made life difficult; when they were forced to move in with Cora's parents, she told him it was time to forget general practice and become a quack. Crippen remained, basically, a quack and a confidence man for the rest of his life. He worked as a salesman for a patent medicine company, and in 1897, became manager of its London office. His employer called himself Professor Munyon, and his cure for piles, advertised by a picture of himself with an upraised finger, gave rise to many ribald jokes. But Munyon fired Crippen when he found he was the "manager" of a music-hall singer — Cora was now calling herself Belle Elmore and was on the stage — and from then on, Crippen was forced to struggle on as a low-grade quack selling worthless nostrums. He became a consultant to a firm of dubious ear specialists, Drovet's, and a magazine editor who called on Crippen had his ears examined with a filthy speculum which he made no attempt to disinfect. He was also startled by Crippen's flamboyant dress — the loud shirt and yellow bow tie, the enormous diamond stick-pin. For a quiet, unassuming little man, Crippen had an odd taste in clothes. He also had a reputation for meanness — he made a habit of offering to buy a drink, then discovering he had left his money at home, and borrowing half a crown. The editor commented on Crippen's "flabby gills and shifty eyes".

The "ear specialist" Drovet went bankrupt when the firm was convicted of gross negligence in the death of a locksmith and other examples of what amounted to medical homicide. But it was there that Crippen met a seventeen-year-old typist named Ethel LeNeve (whose real name was Neave). She was a moaning hypochondriac whose endless complaints of headache and catarrh had earned her the nickname "Not very well thank you". She had been a miserable child, painfully conscious of a deformed foot, and hating her father because he insisted that it would cure itself if she walked properly. (He proved to be right.) She was also jealous of her vivacious younger sister. Yet underneath these unpleasant traits, she had a highly dominant character, and this is undoubtedly what attracted Crippen to her. Crippen was something of a masochist in his relations with women. This is presumably why he did not divorce Cora when he found she had taken an ex-prize-fighter as a lover, and why he put up with a series of lodgers who shared his wife's bed. With bankrupt stock purchased from Drovet's, Crippen set up his own business, with Ethel as his bookkeeper.

As Belle Elmore, Mrs Crippen became a moderate success in the London music-halls. The British liked the American act, and Belle seems to have been the sort of person that everyone liked anyway – immensely vital, good natured, embarrassingly frank. She earned the enduring friendship of Marie Lloyd and many other music-hall artists. But at home, she became inclined to bouts of screaming temper. And most of her friends detested her husband, regarding him as a sponger.

Ethel was in love with her employer, and in some ways they were well suited. Crippen was a crook, although as a result of weakness rather than moral delinquency, and Ethel was a pathological liar, whose biographer Tom Cullen writes that she "lied from sheer perversity – in fact she seemed incapable of telling the truth". But she was also determined not to yield her virginity until they were legally married. It was not until Crippen discovered his wife in bed with the German lodger – and Ethel, presumably, had reason to feel that his marriage was at an end – that she consented to become his wife in the physical sense of the term; the date was 6 December 1906, seven years after their

If the Christine Keeler affair was the great British political scandal of the 1960s, the Max Garvie affair was its equivalent among crimes of passion. Garvie, a wealthy farmer, lived with his wife Sheila and their three children at West Cairnbeg in east Scotland. But when Garvie began to develop an interest in nudism – he founded a local club – pornography, homosexuality and abnormal sex, the marriage began to founder. In 1967, Garvie connived at an affair between his thirty-three-year-old wife and a twenty-two-year-old schoolteacher, Brian Tevendale (to whom he was also attracted). Tevendale in turn introduced Garvie to his married sister, Trudy Birse, who became his mistress, her policeman husband apparently accepting the situation. (At a party, Garvie provided him with a girl, "so the foursome turned into a sextet".) On one occasion, Garvie and Tevendale tossed up to decide who would make love to Sheila first.

When Sheila Garvie and Brian Tevendale ran away together, Garvie was upset and finally persuaded her to return. He paid to have Tevendale beaten-up twice.

On 14 May, 1968, Garvie disappeared after a Scottish National Party meeting. Eventually, Sheila Garvie admitted to her mother that her husband was dead and, after a struggle with her conscience, Mrs Watson went to the police. Garvie's body was discovered in an underground tunnel at Lauriston Castle. Sheila Garvie, Brian Tevendale and Tevendale's friend Alan Peters,

were charged with murdering him by striking
him with a rifle butt or an iron bar.

Mrs Garvie's defence centred on her
husband's sexual perversions, and the
newspapers made the most of the affair, with its
"sixsome" and wife-swopping. The defence did
her no good; a puritanical Scottish jury found
Sheila Garvie and Brian Tevendale guilty, and
they were sentenced to life imprisonment (in
practice, about ten years). Alan Peters was
released on a verdict of "not proven". An
outraged crowd chased Trudy Birse and her
husband down the street, and they had to take
refuge in a newspaper office.

---

first meeting. It seems to have happened in a hired hotel
room during the day, as did their subsequent intimacies –
Crippen continued to return home at night.

Crippen became a dentist, and Ethel his assistant. At one
point, Ethel became pregnant; she was determined to have
the baby, and for a while it looked as if it might transform
their lives, and bring about the inevitable break with Belle.
Then she had a miscarriage. And to make things worse,
Belle went around telling the Music Hall Ladies' Guild
members that no one was sure which of Ethel's many lovers
was responsible. This may well have been the last straw.
Instead of leaving her, which would have been the
obviously sensible course, Crippen decided to murder
her. On 17 January 1910, he bought no fewer than
seventeen grains of hyoscine, a vegetable poison that he
had seen administered to calm the violently insane at
London's Royal Bethlehem Hospital. There is a strong
probability that Ethel knew that her lover intended to kill
his wife – she may even have planned it. On the evening of

Crimes of Passion

31 January 1910, two of Belle's music-hall friends came to dinner at the Crippens' house at 39 Hilldrop Crescent, Camden Town. They said goodbye to Belle at 1.30 the next morning; it was the last time Belle was seen alive. The following day, Crippen pawned Belle's diamond ring and ear-rings, and Ethel slept at Hilldrop Crescent. The following day, letters were received by the Secretary of the Music Hall Guild, signed Belle Elmore and resigning her membership; they explained she was leaving for America to nurse a sick relative. Just before Easter, in the third week of March, Crippen told his friends that Belle was dangerously ill in Los Angeles; soon after, he announced her death.

Belle's friends were suspicious. Someone checked with the shipping lines, and discovered that no one of that name had sailed for America in February. A music-hall performer called Lil Hawthorne paid a visit to New York with her husband John Nash, and they also made enquiries, which achieved no positive result. Back in London, they talked to Crippen, who sobbed convincingly, but told contradictory stories about precisely where Belle had died. The Nashes decided to go to Scotland Yard. There they spoke to Chief Inspector Walter Dew of the CID, who agreed to go and talk to Crippen. And Crippen smoothly admitted that his wife was still alive. She had simply walked out on him and gone to join her former prize-fighter lover in Chicago. Dew was completely taken in. A thorough search of the house convinced him that there were no suspicious circumstances. When Dew left the house, he was more than half convinced that Belle was alive.

Then Crippen made his greatest mistake; he decided to flee. He and Ethel left for Antwerp, and took a ship for Canada. Ethel was dressed as a boy. When Dew returned two days later, and found the house deserted, he called in his team of diggers. Beneath the coal cellar floor, buried in quicklime, he found the remains of Mrs Crippen.

On board the SS *Montrose*, Crippen's secret had already been discovered by Captain Henry Kendal, who quickly realized that "Mr Robinson's" son was a girl in disguise. In a copy of the *Daily Mail* which he had taken on board, the captain found a picture of the wanted "cellar murderer", Crippen. He handed his radio operator a message that began: "Have strong suspicion that Crippen London cellar murderer and accomplice are among saloon passengers." So it came about that Crippen was the first murderer to be caught by means of wireless telegraphy, for which Marconi had received the Nobel prize in the previous year. On the morning of 31 July 1910, as the ship lay off the mouth of the St Lawrence river, Crippen went on deck, and was greeted by Dew, who greeted him with "Good morning, Dr Crippen."

On the morning Cora Crippen's remains were found, Bernard Spilsbury was preparing to leave for a holiday in Minehead with his wife and child. Then he received a summons from his eminent colleagues Drs Pepper, Willcox, and Luff, to go and view the body. Richard Muir, who had prosecuted the Stratton brothers, was in charge of the prosecution. (When Crippen heard this, he remarked dolefully, "I fear the worst.")

Crippen was defended by the brilliant but unscrupulous Arthur Newton, who would later go to prison for forging Crippen's "Confession" and selling it to a newspaper. As a defendant, Crippen was certainly his own worst enemy. His only chance of escaping the rope was to admit everything except intent to kill. But if Crippen pleaded guilty, the whole sordid story about Belle and Ethel would emerge. Crippen chose to protect Ethel and enter a plea of innocence. His defence was that Belle had left him, just as he said, so the body in the cellar must be that of some other woman, buried by some previous tenant, or hidden there during his tenancy. It was obviously an absurd story, and it amounted to suicide. And, of course, it left to the prosecution the fairly light task of proving that the corpse *was* that of Cora Crippen. So the forensic evidence lay at the heart of the case. On one side was the formidable team of Pepper, Willcox, Luff, and Spilsbury, on the other, Drs Turnbull, Wall, and Blyth. Turnbull had been accosted by the defence at a bridge party, and had casually agreed to give his opinion as to whether a piece of skin was from the stomach, and contained an operation scar; he decided it was from a thigh, and that the scar was merely a fold. Since the operation scar was almost enough in itself to identify Mrs Crippen, the defence was delighted. When Arthur Newton broke his promise not to call Turnbull as a witness, the doctor was horrified and tried to change his mind. But unless he was willing to make a public confession of error, it was too late.

Willcox had found hyoscine in the remains, and Crippen was proved to have bought seventeen grains of the drug not long before his wife's disappearance. Spilsbury, an expert on scar tissues, had no doubt whatsoever that the fragment of skin was from a stomach, not a thigh. And when they found part of a rectus muscle of the abdominal wall attached to the skin, the identification was proved beyond doubt. In court, Turnbull identified the skin as coming from the thigh, and the scar as a fold. Spilsbury, with the calm, grave manner that later led juries to think him infallible, pointed out the older man's errors with a pair of forceps, and the harassed Turnbull left the box with an embarrassed flush. He was followed by Dr Wall, who admitted that he had changed his mind about the piece of skin, and that it came from the abdomen. Dr Blyth disputed the presence of hyoscine in the body, but made a poor showing. It was Pepper's team that carried the day, and it was the junior member of that team who made the most powerful impression in court.

Crippen's downfall was not due entirely to this medical team. Part of the body had been wrapped in a piece of pyjamas jacket, and it contained the maker's name. One pair of Crippen's pyjamas had a missing jacket, but Crippen

Ethel LeNeve, disguised as a boy in her attempt to flee across the Atlantic with Dr Crippen.

insisted that these had been purchased years before, in 1905 or 1906 — the intervening years would explain why the jacket was now missing. But Muir was able to establish that the pyjamas to which the jacket belonged had been purchased in 1909. Crippen was caught out in a direct lie, and this did as much as anything to convince the jury of his guilt. It took them only 27 minutes to reach their verdict. Crippen was hanged on 23 November 1910. Ethel was tried separately, but acquitted.

Ethel LeNeve emigrated to Canada, but she returned to England in 1916, took a job in a furniture store in Trafalgar Square, and married an accountant there. Her husband is said to have borne a strong resemblance to Crippen. They lived in East Croydon, and in 1954, she revealed her identity to the novelist Ursula Bloom, who had written a novel called *The Girl Who Loved Crippen*. Miss Bloom became a close friend, and it was to her that Ethel LeNeve remarked one day that she had never ceased to love Crippen. She died in 1967, at the age of eighty-four.

Many writers have pointed out that the great mystery remains: why did Crippen kill his wife when he could simply have walked out of her life? In his novel, *Dr Crippen's Diary*, Emlyn Williams settles for the explanation that Crippen gave her hyoscine tablets in mistake for aspirin. Dr Ingleby Oddie, who worked with Muir for the prosecution, had a more plausible theory. It was his belief that Crippen intended to kill his wife with hyoscine, convinced that her death would be ascribed to a heart attack — which is highly likely. What Crippen did not realize is that a large dose of hyoscine does not invariably act as a sedative, but can have the opposite effect. Witnesses claim to have heard screams coming from 39 Hilldrop Crescent on the morning of the murder, and another neighbour heard a loud bang. Crippen possessed a pistol and ammunition. Oddie speculates that the dose of hyoscine, given in a "night cap", caused her to become hysterical and start screaming. If neighbours rushed in, all Crippen's plans would collapse; there would be an inquest, and hyoscine would be discovered. Crippen salvaged what he could of the murder plan, and shot her through the head — the skull was never found. Then he had no alternative but to dismember the body and seek a place to hide it . . .

Bywaters and Thompson

After the trial of Crippen, the next crime to arouse a comparable sensation was the case of Thompson and Bywaters — in fact, it is arguably the widely publicized *crime passionel* of the period between the two wars.

A little after midnight on 4 October, 1922, a couple were returning to their suburban home in Ilford, Essex, after an evening at the theatre. Suddenly, a man sprang out of the shadows and attacked the husband. The woman was heard to scream: "Oh don't! Oh don't!", but it was too late. Her husband lay on the pavement, and the man ran off into the darkness.

Passers-by helped her and called a doctor; he discovered that the man was already dead. The woman, twenty-eight-year-old Edith Thompson, was escorted home by the police; she was in shock, and told them she had no idea what had happened. Her husband had simply collapsed, she said; she thought he had had one of his heart attacks.

The next morning, the police informed her that her husband, Percy Thompson, had died of number of stab wounds; she still maintained that she had no clear memory of what had happened. But eventually she was able to recall that her husband had been "attacked by a strange man".

By now, the police had heard a name that interested them: Frederick Bywaters, a young man who had once lodged with the Thompsons, but had left after a quarrel with the husband. Percy Thompson's brother, Richard believed that Bywaters — a laundry steward on a P & O liner — was at present at sea. But Superintendent Frederick Wensley, the detective in charge of the case, soon ascertained this was not true. In fact, Bywaters, a young man of twenty, was soon traced to the home of Edith's parents. Brought in for questioning, he seemed arrogant and irritable; in spite of his youth, he was obviously a highly dominant character. But when some spots on the sleeve of his jacket were identified as blood, Wensley informed him that he was going to be detained. He insisted he knew nothing of the death of Percy Thompson.

By this time, the police had obtained a search warrant; and what they found in Edith Thompson's home would eventually condemn her to death: a series of letters written by Edith Thompson to Frederick Bywaters, and signed "Peidi". They made it clear that these two were lovers.

It was Edith who broke first. Crossing the yard at the Ilford police station, she caught a glimpse of Bywaters through the library window. She suddenly cried: "Oh God, what can I do? Why did he do it? I didn't want him to do it. I must tell the truth." And minutes later, in the CID office, she had admitted that the man who stabbed her husband to death was Frederick Bywaters. Soon afterwards, Bywaters also confessed. He admitted waiting for the couple at the end of the road, then grabbing Thompson and asking him to divorce his wife. They grappled, he said, and he pulled out a knife. "He got the worst of it." Mrs Thompson, he insisted, knew nothing about the murder; she had been standing at some distance, "spellbound", at the time . . .

If that had been all, Frederick Bywaters would have hanged alone for the murder of Percy Thompson. But the letters shed an altogether more sinister complexion on the affair. For, if they were to be believed, Edith had been attempting to get rid of her husband by poisoning him with

Dr Arnold Axilrod, a Minneapolis dentist, broke one of the major rules of dental surgeons and often administered anaesthetic to female patients without the presence of a nurse. One seventeen-year-old girl complained that she had been given a pill that knocked her out for several hours.

On 23 April, 1955, the body of twenty-one-year-old Mary Moonen was discovered lying by the side of the road. She had been strangled. Medical examination revealed that she had recently had sexual relations, and that she was three months pregnant. Her husband, a soldier, had been in Korea for more than three months. When it was discovered that Mrs Moonen had had an appointment with Axilrod the evening before, he was arrested.

Axilrod admitted that she had been to see him the previous evening, to tell him she was pregnant, then claimed he had "blacked out". When newspapers reported the case, twenty more women came forward to complain that they had been put to sleep by Dr Axilrod for a period of hours. And Mary Moonen's sister, who had recommended Dr Axilrod to Mary, admitted that Axilrod had anaesthetized her for long periods, then talked "suggestively" to her. "I thought he was kidding."

In court, the prosecution accused Axilrod of habitually having sex with female patients under anaesthetic. Axilrod was sentenced to a period of from five to twenty years in prison.

ground glass – a light bulb pounded into pieces – "big pieces too" – but he had found one of them in his porridge.

The dead man was exhumed, and his stomach examined – by Bernard Spilsbury – for signs of poisoning with powdered glass. Spilsbury concluded that Edith's account was pure imagination.

Nevertheless, when the trial opened on 6 December 1922, Edith Thompson stood beside her lover in the dock. The jury heard how, in the summer of the previous, year – 1921 – the love affair had started on holiday on the Isle of Wight. The Thompsons had gone there with Edith's younger sister, Avis Graydon, and her boyfriend Freddy Bywaters, who was a friend of her brother's. Edith had known him since he was a schoolboy (even now he was only eighteen).

Edith had married Percy Thompson when she was twenty-two, in 1915; her husband, a shipping clerk was two years her senior. Percy had joined the London Scottish Regiment, and his wife, who was a romantic young woman, inclined to hysteria, had taken to her bed. However, Thompson proved to have heart trouble, and was soon invalided out. Thompson seems to have been dull but reliable, and his pay was poor; in fact, Edith contributed more to the family budget with her pay as the manageress of a millinery firm in the City, for which she received the generous (for 1922) salary of £6 a week.

It seems that the lovers were first attracted to one another on the Isle of Wight holiday, and when Bywaters kissed Edith, she made no protest. But Thompson noticed nothing of the flirtation – he probably regarded Bywaters as little more than a child – and liked the young man enough to suggest that he come and lodge with them. Freddy accepted the suggestion, and a week later told Edith he was in love with her. They sealed their love with a kiss – but, at this stage, went no further.

Two months later – in August – Percy Thompson realized that he had made a mistake in inviting Bywaters

Mrs Thompson with Frederick Bywaters.

to live with them. The young man was unmistakably sweet on Edith, and she encouraged him by allowing him to fetch and carry for her. In fact, this was what led to the quarrel that caused Freddy Bywaters to leave their home. One warm afternoon, as they sat in the garden waiting for the arrival of Avis Graydon, Edith, who was sewing, asked for a pin. Bywaters rushed in to get one. Percy Thompson was in a grumpy mood, and made some sarcastic remark about her desire to have people at her beck and call. The two began to bicker. Later, at tea, (Avis was late) Thompson continued to be grumpy, and made some critical remarks about Edith's family. In the garden, Freddy heard a crash as a chair overturned, and a gasp of pain from Edith as she was thrown across the room. Bywaters made the mistake of interfering, and was told to pack his bags and get out.

How the love affair continued is not clear — except that the lovers now had to meet secretly. Neither is it known when she cast aside her inhibitions and became the young man's mistress. But from 9 September, Bywaters was away at sea, and "Peidi" wrote to him at every opportunity ("darling your old pal is getting quite a sport. On Saturday I was first in the Egg and Spoon race and first in the 100-yard Flat race and third in the 50-yards last race . . .") When he returned, they began to meet secretly again. Percy Thompson, now thoroughly suspicious, waited at the station one day, and saw Edith get off the train with Bywaters. He waited until later, at home, to upbraid her, sneering that Bywaters had seen him at the station and "run away". When Edith reported this aspersion to her lover, he lost no time in calling at the house and insisting that he had not run away — he had simply not seen Thompson. When Bywaters told Percy Thompson that he was making Edith's life hell, the husband replied with asperity: "I've got her and I'll keep her."

In November Bywaters went back to sea in the *Morea*, and there were more letters. Thompson wanted his wife to have a baby; she refused angrily. Then she suddenly decided she preferred domestic peace, and told her lover that she had given way and "surrendered to him unconditionally" — a phrase that sounds as if it was intended to arouse jealousy. Now the letters begin to contain day-dreams of getting rid of her husband. How about poisoned chocolates? Or hyoscine, the drug Crippen had used? She might poison him with gas if they had gas in the house . . . But perhaps a ground electric light bulb would serve just as well? Or an overdose of opium? It was soon after this that she told her lover that she had tried powdered glass three times, but that she had decided to give up these attempts at murder after her husband found a large piece of glass in his porridge; further attempts could wait until Bywaters returned. She reassured Bywaters that if Percy died, there would be no suspicion because of his bad heart.

The *Morea* was away on a long voyage – to Australia – so Edith had plenty of time to daydream. But finally – on 23 September, 1922 – the long wait was over. They met at a restaurant opposite her office in Aldersgate Street. On Saturday morning she got time off from work and they spent the morning in the park. They even seem to have found an opportunity to make love, for she writes tenderly about "what happened last night".

She was remorseful about going to the theatre with her husband, and advised her lover to "do something to make you forget" – perhaps take Avis out. "I'll be hurt I know, but I want you to hurt me – I do really . . ."

In fact, Bywaters spent the evening with her parents in Upper Norwood. Then, with a sheath knife in his pocket, he had made his way to Ilford to meet them on their return from the theatre . . .

This, then, was the evidence presented before Mr Justice Shearman, who was clearly horrified by the letters and all they implied. "Right-minded persons will be filled with disgust", he told the jury. The Solicitor General, Sir Thomas Inskip, who presented the case for the prosecution, found it an easy task to convince the jury that Edith Thompson was a wicked and abandoned woman who had planned the murder of her husband. The letters – presented by the prosecution in telling but misleading extracts – left no doubt of it. Edith spoke in her own defence, alleging that that she was deliberately misleading her lover into thinking she wanted to kill her husband when her real motive was to keep his love. (She might have been more honest if she had said "keep him interested".)

Frederick Bywaters at the inquest on the death of Mr Thompson,
whom he had stabbed to death with the aid of Thompson's wife.

After a hostile summing-up from the judge, the jury took only two hours to find both defendants guilty. When Mr Justice Shearman read aloud the death sentence, Edith cried: "I am not guilty. Oh God, I am not guilty." The date of the execution was set for 6 January, 1923. Three days before this, Bywaters told his mother that although *he* was guilty and deserved to hang, Edith had no idea he intended to attack her husband that night. But a last minute appeal — based on this "confession" — to the Home Secretary was rejected only hours before the execution. Both were hanged at precisely 9 a.m., she in Holloway, he in Pentonville. Edith Thompson was in such a state of collapse that she had to be carried to the scaffold.

Was she guilty? Certainly not of planning the events of the night of 4 October. But although the sixty-two letters fail to prove that she really intended her husband to die, they leave no doubt that it was she who put the idea of killing Percy Thompson into her lover's head. Her letters about ground glass and poison, whether fantasy or not, undoubtedly convinced Frederick Bywaters that Percy Thompson had to die. Whether or not that constitutes guilt must be left to the judgement of the reader.

Chapter Five

Early 20th-Century Crimes of Passion

C rimes of passion murders are committed all over the world, even following the same pattern, without there being a connection between the cases except in the fact that they are similar in genre. In the early twentieth century, the American equivalent of the Bywaters and Thompson murder was the Hall-Mills case; it became the great American cause célèbre of the 1920s. And another case, although murder is not a humorous subject, aroused universal hilarity due to the fact that the wife's lover lived in various attics throughout their fifteen-year love affair.

The Hall-Mills Murders

O n 16 September 1922, a courting couple taking a stroll near Brunswick, New Jersey, came upon two corpses in a country lane. They proved to be those of the local minister Edward Wheeler Hall, who was forty-one, and of one of his choir singers, Mrs Eleanor Mills, thirty-four. Scattered around the bodies were various torn letters, and the minister's calling card was propped against one of his feet. Both had been shot dead; the woman's throat had been cut from ear to ear, and her tongue and vocal cords removed. The letters proved to be love letters from Mrs Mills to the Reverend Hall, and proved conclusively that she had been his mistress for some time.

Clearly, this was a *crime passionnel*, and all the evidence pointed towards the minister's wife Frances, seven years his senior, and her two brothers Willie and Henry – the latter was an expert shot. But quarrels between two lots of country police about their jurisdiction, and incredible official bungling, finally led a Grand Jury to decide that there was insufficient evidence to charge anyone with the murders.

Four years later, the case was reopened when the husband of a parlourmaid in the minister's household tried to get his marriage annulled, and made some amazing accusations. Arthur Riehl stated that the parlourmaid, Louise Geist, had learned that the minister and his mistress had planned to elope, and had passed on this information to Mrs Hall. On the night of the murder, Mrs Hall, her brother Willie, and Louise Geist drove out to the lovers' lane where the couple planned to meet, and killed the two of them. Louise received $5,000 for her part in the crime and for her silence. The newspapers made the accusation into front-page headlines, and Mrs Hall and her brothers were arrested.

Some of the most telling evidence against them came from a bizarre lady who became known as the Pig Woman; she was Mrs Jane Gibson, who ran a pig farm near De Russey's Lane, the scene of the murder, and who claimed that at 10.30 on the night of 14 September 1922, she had passed close to the crab apple tree under which the bodies were later found, and heard a quarrel, followed by shots. But the Pig Woman's mother, who was also in court, insisted that her daughter was a pathological liar. During the trial, the Pig Woman collapsed – she proved to be suffering from cancer – and had to give her evidence from a hospital bed in the courtroom.

But the most impressive evidence concerned the visiting card propped by the dead man's foot. It had been in a safe in the State Prosecutor's office since the day after the murder.

Crimes of Passion

And when examined in the Middlesex County fingerprint laboratory, it had been found to contain a fingerprint. Lieutenant Fred Drewen mounted the stand and testified that he had taken the fingerprints of Willie Stevens, and that the print on the visiting card was that of Stevens's left index finger. Next, the head of the Bureau of Records of the Newark Police Department, Edward H. Schwartz, testified that he had examined the card and found that the fingerprint on it was that of Willie Stevens. Finally, Joseph Faurot, who had ended as New York's Deputy Police Commissioner, mounted the stand. He not only testified that the fingerprint was that of Willie Stevens, but produced transparencies of the accused man's fingerprints, which he projected on a screen, explaining to the jury his reasons for having no doubt. In an English or French court of law, that would have settled the case; unless Willie Stevens could explain how his fingerprints came to be on the minister's calling card, the jury would have concluded that it was he who had placed the card against the dead man's foot.

Fortunately for the defendants, there was a dramatic interruption; Alexander Simpson, the prosecutor, announced that the Pig Woman was at death's door, and about to sink into a coma. So Faurot stood down to make room for the Pig Woman's doctor, and the judge announced that the trial would be adjourned for the time being.

Back on the stand a few days later, Schwartz and Faurot again insisted that the fingerprint on the card was that of Willie Stevens, although they agreed that being exposed to the weather for thirty-six hours might have impaired the print.

When the maid, Louise Geist, appeared on the stand, she testified that, on the morning after the murder, Willie had told her that "something terrible happened last night". And another witness, Marie Demarest, told how a private detective hired by Mrs Hall had tried to bribe her to suppress part of her testimony.

Things looked black for the defendants. Yet, incredibly, the defence made no real attempt to discredit the most serious piece of evidence: the calling card. Robert J. McCarter told the jury: "I charge with all the solemnity that is involved in it that the card is a fraud." But he made no attempt to explain how a fraudulent fingerprint could be fabricated, or how, if the card itself was a fraud, Willie Stevens had been induced to put his fingerprint on it. The jury was apparently incurious about this vital point. On 3 December 1926, after deliberating for five hours, they returned a verdict of not guilty. James Mills, the sexton and husband of the murdered woman, remarked that he was not surprised, since money could buy anything . . .

At this distance in time, the solution to this "unsolved" murder case seems obvious. The defence was correct about one thing: Frances Hall had no idea that Eleanor Mills was her husband's mistress. When she found out — probably from overhearing a telephone conversation about an elopement — she summoned her brothers, and they hurried off to administer summary justice. Mrs Hall may have been doubly enraged because she genuinely liked Eleanor Mills and had always treated her with kindness. If the Pig Woman's testimony is correct, Hall was shot first, above the ear, while Eleanor ran away; they found her with the aid of a torch, dragged her back and shot her beside her lover. Then the infuriated wife slit her throat and removed the vocal cords that had been responsible for the sweet voice that had seduced her husband.

Then why was she acquitted, when all the evidence pointed to her guilt? The answer may lie in the flamboyant manner of the prosecuting counsel, a native of Jersey City, who had referred to the residents of Somerset County, where the trial took place, as country bumpkins. During the trial, his extrovert city manners evidently grated on the jury. It seems probable that the verdict was a gesture of defiance and contempt towards State Senator Alexander Simpson rather than an affirmation of belief in the innocence of Mrs Hall and her brothers.

The Walburger Case

This case adds a touch of humour to crime, as the murderer takes on the ingenious disguise of a ghost.

As early as 1908, Bert Walburger, an overweight Minneapolis cabinet-maker, suspected that his wife Dotty was having an affair with a sixteen year old employee of a paint and varnish company named Gus Huberman. This seemed to suggest that the rather plain young woman was sex starved — or starved for romance — for Huberman was slight and pale, with a receding chin. Or perhaps the youth aroused her maternal instinct, for she had recently lost her own eight year old son, and Huberman was an orphan. A private detective hired by the jealous husband rushed back one day to report that Huberman and Dotty Walburger had taken a train to Chicago. Attempts to track them down were a failure, but Dotty soon returned of own accord; she admitted her infidelity and asked for a divorce. Her husband refused, on the grounds that his alimony would benefit "that shrimp".

Three years later, in 1911, Walburger decided that his rival had left town, and dismissed the private detective. In fact, Gus Huberman was by then spending most of his nights in the bed of their deceased son Raymond, and his days in the bed of Dotty Walburger. Eventually, he moved into the attic room in the Walburger's house, rendered confident by the knowledge that Walburger was too corpulent to climb the ladder and scramble through the trapdoor.

One day, Bert Walburger looked up from the garden, and saw Gus Huberman's face looking down at him. Dotty told

In March 1948, James Camb, a deck steward on a liner, was tried for the murder of an attractive passenger, actress Gay Gibson. The unusual feature of the case was that Gay Gibson's body was never recovered. Her cabin on the liner, Durban Castle, had been found empty on the morning of 18 October, 1947, and it was at first assumed that she had fallen overboard. Then a watchman stated that in the early hours of the morning, someone had pushed the bell in her cabin, and that when he went to answer it, James Camb had opened the door.

Questioned by the police, Camb stated that he had been invited to Gay Gibson's cabin, and that she had received him wearing only a dressing gown. He claimed that, in the act of sexual intercourse, she had been foaming at the mouth and then died. When the watchman had knocked at the door, he had panicked and pushed her body out of the porthole.

The fact that urine stains on the bedsheets suggested strangulation, and the girl's pyjamas were missing (suggesting that she had been wearing them when pushed out of the porthole) led the jury to find Camb guilty; he was sentenced to life imprisonment.

him he was imagining things, and he reluctantly decided he must be suffering from overwork. During the day, Gus would make love to Dotty and help her with the housework. He was a combination of pet, houseboy and stallion. Meanwhile, Bert Walburger's business had become so prosperous that he now owned a factory that employed fifteen hundred people; Gus later claimed that his advice, passed on to Bert via his wife, had saved the business on a number of critical occasions.

Up in his attic, Gus listened in to the life that went on below. Admittedly, Sundays in summer were too hot, and on winter nights, he had to struggle to avoid coughs and sneezes, and had to learn to move as silently as a mouse. Yet life was smooth and pleasant enough, and he was neither sex starved nor underfed.

Bert's increasing prosperity led them to change house a number of times; when that happened, Dotty had to smuggle Gus into the attic again. There he spent his days reading Dickens, Mark Twain and any old magazines Dotty could provide. She also provided him with pocket money, but he had little opportunity to spend it.

During World War I, Gus announced that he was going to fight for his country; Dotty's tears and pleas dissuaded him – temporarily. Finally, patriotism triumphed, and he went and enlisted. The sergeant's jibes about his size sent him scurrying back to his attic within hours. Now he was a deserter, he made doubly sure that no one suspected his presence.

Soon after that, Bert decided to retire, and the Walburgers moved out to Los Angeles. Gus went on ahead, and hung around until they arrived. He was trailing them as they went house-hunting in Los Angeles. Dotty rejected several houses because they had no attic. Finally, the Walburgers found a suitable place, and Gus moved into his fifth attic in fourteen years.

The end came some months later, on 29 August, 1922. Neighbours heard shots, and a woman screaming. They rang the police, who had to break into the house through the bolted front door. Bert Walburger was lying dead on the floor, shot through the head with a .25, a lady-size gun. Dotty Walburger was found locked in the closet in her locked bedroom. She told how she was getting undressed in the clothes closet when she heard shots; then the closet door was locked behind her. That was all she could tell them . . .

At first, nothing seemed to be missing. Then Dotty recalled her husband's diamond studded watch, and the large bank roll he habitually carried around. This must obviously have been the burglar's objective. The investigation soon reached a dead end. The house proved to be full of fingerprints that the police were unable to identify, but whoever the burglar was, he had no criminal record.

A year later, the diamond-studded watch turned up – in the waistcoat pocket of an accountant named Sol Shephard. He was Mrs Walburger's accountant, and he said she had given him the watch. Dotty confirmed this – she had found the watch under a mat, and had only failed to notify the police because she imagined they were no longer interested.

A neighbour now came forward to offer evidence that seemed to incriminate Mrs Walburger – he told how, soon after the murder, she had asked him to destroy a small revolver by filing it into small pieces. He had dumped these into a tar sump. An enterprising newspaper succeeded in recovering the pieces. Then another neighbour of the Walburgers described how Dotty had asked *him* to dispose of yet another revolver soon after the murder. This was also finally located. It began to look as if Dotty Huberman *could* have killed her husband, then, with a certain amount of ingenuity, locked herself in the closet.

Mrs Walburger was questioned for days. But eventually, the police had to release her. However, before they did this, Mrs Walburger asked to see her accountant, Mr Sol Shepherd . . .

Eight years later, in 1930, Mr Shepherd went to the police and told them that his conscience was troubling him. When he had spoken to Mrs Walburger, she had told him that her dissolute younger brother was living in the attic of her home. Would he please go there, scratch on the wall, and take him food and water? Sol Shepherd did as she asked, and was confronted by a small man with a receding chin, who admitted that he had been living in various attics for years. But he admitted he was tired of his situation, and was anxious to leave. Besides, if the police found him now, it would incriminate Mrs Walburger. So Shepherd drove Gus Huberman to the main highway to San Francisco, and Gus finally detached himself from his mistress of fifteen years.

The police searched Dotty Walburger's former home — she had moved by now to a smaller residence — and found that the attic showed signs of long-time habitation. Soon after that, Gus Huberman was arrested. He was now married, and was working as the caretaker of an apartment building.

Back at the police station, Huberman admitted shooting Bert Walburger. But, he said, it had been an accident. Ever since the Walburger home had been burgled, he had kept a revolver close to hand. That night in August, he had heard the Walburgers returning from an evening out, then quarrelling. Bert had slapped his wife so hard she fell down. So he, Gus, had hastened downstairs, to find Bert Walburger standing over his prostrate wife. When Bert saw his rival, he exploded: "You little rat! What are you doing here?" There was a scuffle, and the gun had gone off. When the struggle was over, Bert Walburger lay dead, and Mrs Walburger was wailing: "Gee this is terrible!" Then Gus saw the answer: lock Dotty in her closet, then lock the bedroom door and retreat to his own attic . . .

The five week trial of Gus Huberman caused a sensation; the story of the "Phantom Lover in the Attic" gripped the imagination of America. But a moving speech from Gus's attorney, Earl Wakeman, ensured the sympathy of the jury for the poor orphan. They decided that he was guilty only of manslaughter, and Gus received a sentence of three years. The truth was, nobody had the heart to see him executed. And since the death of Bert Walburger had taken place eight years earlier, a statute of limitations meant that he was free. He went back to his wife and their apartment building.

Dotty Walburger was tried separately. But when the jury failed to reach an agreement, the DA decided he couldn't face it all over again, and begged to be excused. Mrs Walburger also walked free. She retired to a small apartment, and lived there peacefully until her death.

Death at the Savoy

In September 1923, after a passionate appeal by the famous advocate Marshall Hall, a British jury acquitted a Frenchwoman who had shot her Egyptian husband to death. It appears to demonstrate that even the British are capable of recognizing that the perpetrator of a *crime passionel* may not be legally guilty. However, this was a case in which the killer hardly deserved clemency.

Madame Fahmy was thirty-three years old, and in the previous year she had married Prince Ali Kemal Fahmy Bey, a handsome and wealthy Egyptian playboy who was ten years her junior. He had fallen violently in love with Marguerite Laurent shortly after she had divorced her previous husband. The prince pursued her to Deauville, where she became his mistress. In December 1922 she became a Moslem, and they were married. But the marriage was unhappy. Madame Fahmy might look slender and vulnerable, but she had a violent temper, and was unaccustomed to being bossed around. Prince Fahmy, on the other hand, had an oriental prejudice in favour of obedient females. The two often clashed violently, and on one occasion he locked her in her cabin for twenty-four hours. "With women", he said, "one must act with energy and be severe." The prince also had a male secretary, Said

Ernani, with whom he was rumoured to have a homosexual relationship.

On 9 July, 1923, the Fahmy's were staying at London's Savoy Hotel, and having a disagreement about some minor operation which she needed; she wanted to go to Paris and he wanted her to have it in London. At dinner there was a violent disagreement, and the princess was heard to say (in French – she spoke no English): "You shut up or I'll smash this bottle over your head." When the bandleader asked her if there was any tune she would like to hear, she replied: "I don't want any music – my husband threatened to kill me tonight." The maestro bowed politely and said: "I hope you will still be here tomorrow, madame." Later, her husband asked her to dance but she refused; clearly, Madame Fahmy was by no means under the thumb of her husband.

At about 1.30 that following morning, a porter was passing their suite when the prince came out in his pyjamas. "Look what she has done", he said, indicating a red scratch on his cheek. Madame Fahmy, still in evening dress, came out of the room, and said something the porter did not understand. He warned them that they might wake the other guests, and they went back into the room. As the porter turned away, a little dog ran out, and the prince bent down and whistled for it, snapping his fingers. A few moments later, three shots rang out. The porter ran back to the open door and saw Madame Fahmy throwing down a pistol, and her husband lying on the floor and bleeding from the head. A few hours later the prince died in hospital, and Madame Fahmy was arrested. Her trial opened less than two weeks later, on 23 July, 1923.

One thing that seems perfectly clear is that if the prince treated his wife badly, she was able to give as good as she got. But her advocate, Edward Marshall Hall, based his defence on the notion of a poor, oppressed woman who had made the mistake of marrying a despotic oriental of perverted sexual tastes, who often beat and kicked her.

In fact, the secretary denied that his master had ever kicked her, although he admitted that the prince had once hit his wife so violently that he had dislocated her jaw.

The manager of the Savoy, giving evidence, described how Madame Fahmy had said to him, in French: "I lost my head." Marshall Hall suggested that a better translation of "J'ai perdu la tete" would be: "I was frightened out of my wits." The manager agreed.

The firearms expert, Robert Churchill, testified that although the pistol with which Fahmy was shot was an automatic, the trigger had to be pulled for each shot.

The jury was sent out while Marshall Hall asked the judge to rule against the prosecution, who wanted to question Madame Fahmy about her relations with other men, to prove she was an immoral woman. This, Marshall Hall said, would prejudice the jury against her. He made no attempt to deny that the allegations were true. Nevertheless, the judge ruled in his favour.

In a dramatic final speech, Marshall Hall described Madame Fahmy, crouching like a terrified animal, with the gun in her hands, and then the weapon exploding — to her horror and consternation. He enacted the scene, pointing the gun at the jury, then dropping it dramatically. "Members of the Jury, I want you to open the doors so this Western woman can go out . . ." he declaimed, in a flagrant appeal to racial prejudice. But they were convinced, and took a little over an hour to acquit her.

That dramatic final scene, of course, did not and could not have taken place. A few moments before his death, Prince Fahmy was whistling for a little dog; the porter had only walked a few yards when the shots rang out — three of them. The firing of the gun was obviously no accident — she pressed the trigger three times. But a sentimental British jury preferred to believe that a pretty Frenchwoman killed her husband when she was in a state of terror. (Marshall Hall made doubly sure of an acquittal by hinting that the quarrel was really about the prince's desire for anal sex, which his wife had refused.) So Madame Fahmy walked free, and went on to become a film star, playing the part of an Egyptian wife.

In the previous year, a British jury had sentenced an obviously innocent woman — Edith Thompson — to hang; now another jury acquitted a woman who was obviously guilty. C'est la vie.

Ruth Snyder

The Snyder and Grey case was responsible for one of the most macabre images of the 1920s — the photograph of Ruth Snyder at the moment she was electrocuted, taken by a reporter with a camera strapped to his ankle.

Ruth's crime — planning the death of her husband — had a precedent in the previous decade. In 1919, a Cleveland housewife had hired two Italian thugs to murder her husband, publisher Daniel D. Kaber, who was confined to his bed following a stroke. Kaber's father was convinced that his daughter-in-law Eva was responsible, but there was no evidence against her. He hired Pinkerton detectives, who were able to prove that Eva had hired two "hit men" named Pisselli and Calla for $5,000. Eva Kaber and her two accomplices were all sentenced to life imprisonment.

A fourteen-year-old Swedish girl named Ruth Brown (her father had anglicized his name from Sorensen) undoubtedly read about the case, for Mrs Kaber was living in New York when she was arrested by a detective named Arthur Carey, and the story made headlines. Photographs show a remarkable resemblance between Eva Kaber and Ruth Brown — or Ruth Snyder, as she became. And when Ruth Snyder made up her mind that her own husband had

Even in France, *crime passionel* does not always result in acquittal.

In 1951, Leone Bouvier, a peasant girl of St-Macaire-en-Mauges, met a car mechanic named Emile Clenet at a dance, and soon became his mistress. An unattractive girl, who had been brought up in extreme poverty, she craved affection – a characteristic of which several unscrupulous males had already taken advantage. They began meeting regularly on Sundays in a hotel bedroom. When she became pregnant, Clenet told her to procure an abortion; she did, but it made her ill and cost her her factory job. When Clenet then refused to see her again, she purchased a pistol. Seeing Clenet emerging from a cinema, she persuaded him to take her to a carnival, where he admitted to her that he intended to emigrate to North Africa. That night, in the midst of a farewell embrace, she shot him through the head, then went to join her sister in a convent.

Tried in December 1953, it took a jury only a quarter of an hour to find her guilty of murder. She was sentenced to life imprisonment.

to die, she decided on a less obvious method than hiring two thugs.

Ruth, born in 1895, was brought up in conditions of considerable poverty on 125th Street and Morningside, on the West side. She became a telephone operator when she was thirteen, then a stenographer. Life continued to be hard.

In 1914, she was still a telephone operator. One day she mis-routed a call, and was irritably upbraided by the man on the other end. She apologized so charmingly that he rang back and said he was sorry; they conversed, and he introduced himself as Albert Schneider, the art editor of *Motor Boat*, a Hearst publication; he told her that if she wanted a better job, he could probably provide one. Ruth took him up on the offer, and went to work as a secretary for *Motor Boat* in September. Schneider found the blue-eyed blonde delicious, and before Christmas, had proposed. It seems to have been the diamond that she found in a box of chocolates that led her to accept. They were married in the following July, when she was twenty and her husband thirty-three.

It was not a happy marriage. Their temperaments were unsympathetic. Schneider (he was to change his name to Snyder a few years later in deference to the anti-German feeling caused by the war) was a calm, efficient man of somewhat dominant character — he had been known to overturn a table and stalk out of a restaurant when the waiter displeased him — who needed a good hausfrau; Ruth, whose life had been starved of excitement, wanted to dance, to visit restaurants and holiday resorts, and to play bridge. She found life as a housewife in Queens, Long Island, a bore, and she enlivened it with bridge and luncheon parties. In 1918 she gave birth to a daughter, Lorraine, but it failed to improve her marriage; Albert Snyder made it clear that he found fatherhood tiresome.

For the next seven years they continued to quarrel and lead virtually separate lives — Snyder usually came home late, then read the paper until bedtime. Ruth moved her mother in with them to act as baby-sitter, and continued to do as she liked; what this was, we can only guess from the fact that a notebook found in her home contained the names of twenty-eight men.

These names included that of Henry Judd Grey, a rather quiet little corset salesman who wore thick tortoise-shell spectacles. Ruth had been introduced to him in a cheap

Swedish diner in New York in June 1925. A few weeks later, after a quarrel with her husband, she returned from vacation on Shelter Island with her daughter, and went to dine with Judd Grey. After the meal, they called in at Grey's office, where Ruth complained of her sunburned shoulders. Grey immediately produced a remedy called camphor ice, which he rubbed on her shoulders. Ruth burst into tears, explaining that she was unaccustomed to such courtly behaviour. Judd kissed her. Then he offered her a corselet as a gift and, with an audacity probably due to drink, offered to fit it there and then. Whether their lovemaking continued on the office floor, or in some nearby hotel, is unknown; what is certain is that Ruth began spending nights with him in hotels, and that her husband accepted her explanation that she was staying with a friend. He even made no objection when she invented a friend in Albany and went off there for several days.

They seem to have been an odd pair. Grey was of English puritan stock, and he was puritanical by nature, as well as mild and gentle. He is certainly one of the most unlikely murderers in criminal history. Ruth was undoubtedly the more dominant of the two. But then, Grey seemed to enjoy being dominated – he liked to embrace her ankles, and called her "Momsie". And the more they made love, the more he wanted her. In fact, he was already married, to a girl who would have suited Albert Snyder down to the ground, a "home girl" whose major virtue was that she was "a careful and exceptionally exact housekeeper". Unfortunately, Isabel Gray and Albert Snyder never seem to have met.

Grey's salary was considerably smaller than that of Albert Snyder, and his new role as a lover demanded more money than he earned. Ruth seems to have lent – or given – him a number of sums, including a cheque for $200.

It is not clear why Ruth Snyder decided to kill her husband rather than simply running away with Judd Grey.

But it is on record that, soon after Ruth became Grey's mistress, Albert Snyder narrowly escaped death on a number of occasions. One evening, when he was tinkering underneath the car, the jack slipped and he was almost crushed to death. Possibly this was an accident — an accident that made Ruth realize how convenient it would have been if Albert *had* been crushed. Not long after this, Snyder was running the car engine in the garage when Ruth brought him a glass of whiskey. It made him oddly dizzy, so that he hardly noticed when the garage door closed. He was almost unconscious from carbon monoxide fumes when he succeeded in staggering outside.

Yet, although Albert Snyder told his brother that he thought his wife had tried to kill him, he nevertheless accepted her suggestion that he should insure his life. Perhaps he thought that no harm would come to him for the sake of a mere $1,000. In fact, the thousand dollar policy which he signed in triplicate was actually three policies, whose total amounted to more than $100,000. It was Ruth who paid the premiums.

A few months later, in July 1926, Albert Snyder awoke from a doze on the settee gasping for air; the room was full of coal gas. Ruth explained that she must have accidentally stepped on the tube connecting the gas cock to the fire, and pulled it off. In the following January she gave Albert a medicine to cure hiccups; it was not Alka-Seltzer but bichloride of mercury, and made him seriously ill.

When Ruth first raised the subject of killing her husband, Grey was deeply shocked. But as time went by, he became accustomed to it. To begin with, he thought it was idle talk. But when she announced, in September 1926, that she had definitely decided to kill Albert, Grey told her she ought to have her head examined. Still, he was interested enough to ask her how she intended to do it, and listened with fascination to her plan to knock her husband unconscious with a sleeping powder, then turn on the gas. In the following month, when she asked him to help her in killing her husband, he blenched and told her she was foolish to entertain such ideas. But when she emphasized how much she hated having sex with her husband, and how often he demanded his marital rights, he began to waver.

It seems absurd that, after so much planning, the murder itself was almost criminally incompetent. Grey, who had been drinking heavily to give himself courage, entered the house late on the evening of 20 March, 1927, and hid himself to await their return from a party. Ruth's mother was away, and Grey concealed himself in her bedroom. There he drank more whiskey.

At 2 a.m. the Snyders returned, together with eight-year-old Lorraine, who had also been to the party. Ruth was sober, but she had made sure that her husband had drunk more than enough. By 2.30, Snyder was asleep, and Ruth had sneaked out of her twin bed to summon her lover. Judd entered their bedroom carrying a sash weight, and took an almighty swing at the head of the sleeping man. In his excitement he missed, grazing Snyder's skull, and the intended victim was shocked awake. Grey hit him again, then staggered as Snyder punched him — Snyder, the boating fantatic, was far bigger than Grey. They struggled, and as Grey tried to free his necktie from Snyder's powerful grip, he dropped the sashweight. "Momsie, help me!" he gasped, and Ruth found the sash weight and hit her husband on the back of the head. Albert Snyder went limp.

The lovers now stuffed chloroform-soaked rags into Snyder's mouth and nostrils, then wound picture-wire around his throat so that it cut in deeply. Already, they were overdoing it — no burglar would have gone to so much trouble after knocking his victim unconscious. They then disarranged the furniture to lend weight to the burglar story, and pulled open the drawers. Grey changed into one of his victim's shirts — his own was bloodstained — and finally left, after tying her hands and ankles and binding a gag around her mouth. He declined her request to knock her unconscious, which proved to be another major mistake.

Lorraine Snyder was awakened by a tapping on her bedroom door, and opened it to find her mother lying on the floor, her wrists and ankles still bound. Ruth told her to summon the neighbours, and the child ran across the street to awaken Mr and Mrs Mulhauser. The latter found that Ruth had untied her hands, but not her ankles. Among the police who were summoned was Detective Arthur Carey, who had arrested Mrs Kaber seven years earlier. And Carey, like the young doctor who had preceded him, instantly smelt a rat. Ruth claimed that she had been attacked by a big man with a moustache, but failed to explain how she saw him in the dark. The doctor had already observed that she was unbruised and showed no other sign of rough handling. Carey decided that no professional burglar (or burglars) would have knocked Snyder unconscious, then chloroformed him and strangled him with picture wire; this was obviously the work of someone who wished him dead. And surely Ruth would have untied her own ankles after she had freed her hands, not waited for the Mulhauers to arrive? The sheer disorder of the house also suggested that the "burglary" had been staged by enthusiastic amateurs. A gun left on the bed also aroused Carey's suspicions — surely burglars would not have left it behind when Ruth might have freed herself and pursued them with a volley of shots? Finally, the blood-stained sash weight was found in the tool chest; why should a burglar go to the trouble of concealing it when he could simply drop it on the floor?

As the interrogation continued, Ruth was left in no doubt that the police knew she was lying. She stubbornly denied this, and also denied — what was equally obvious — that she must have had an accomplice. With typical incompetence, Grey had left behind a tie pin with his initials; Ruth explained that J.G. stood for Jessie Guishard, her husband's previous fiancée, who had died, and to begin with, the police believed her. But when they found the notebook containing the names of twenty-eight men, and found that of Judd Grey among them, they lost no time jumping to the correct conclusion. And when the cancelled cheque for $200 was found – made out to Judd Grey – Ruth finally began to look worried. But still she persisted in her story about the rough man with the black moustache.

After more than twelve hours of questioning, she was removed to the police station, and there she was told that Judd Grey had confessed. It was untrue – he had not even been found – but it convinced her. Believing herself betrayed, she felt outraged. So when Police Commissioner McLaughlin stated: "Grey helped to kill your husband, didn't he?", she answered defiantly: "Yes."

The rest was predictable. Grey was arrested at half past midnight in the Onondaga Hotel, Syracuse. He had already told a friend that he had been in Ruth's house when two burglars had broken in and attacked Ruth and her husband; he said he had hidden in a closet until they had gone. The friend had obligingly disposed of some bloodstained clothes. Now Grey told the police that he had not even been in the Snyders' house that night. But when the police told him they had found the train ticket that proved he had travelled from Syracuse to Long Island, he admitted it quietly. By now, Ruth Snyder's confession was in all the headlines. Grey went on to tell the whole story, omitting no detail.

The trial lasted from 18 April, 1927, to 9 May. Ruth Snyder's defence blamed Judd Grey; Judd Grey's defence blamed Ruth Snyder. Ruth insisted that Grey had overpowered her and killed her husband; Grey was more chivalrous, but there was no doubt that he blamed his mistress. The jury reached a unanimous verdict of guilty – no other was possible – and both were sentenced to death.

Grey went to his death calmly and philosophically on 12 January, 1928. Ruth died hard; a few days before her execution she began to scream for hours every night. Like Edith Thompson, she had to be half-carried to her death. A reporter on the New York *Daily News* had a camera strapped to his ankle, with a shutter release in his pocket. As all eyes were fixed on the straining body, hurled against the straps by the powerful current, he stepped into the aisle and raised his trouser leg. The picture was published the following morning over the whole front page of the *Daily News*; it was subsequently syndicated all over the world.

The Ruxton Case

The commonest motive for the *crime passionel* is jealousy. But most such murders are committed in hot blood, and in about one third of all such cases, the murderer commits suicide. This explains why so few jealousy-murders are to be found in books such as this; the details are usually so commonplace that there is virtually no story.

The Ruxton case is one of the most striking exceptions. 29 September, 1935, was a cool autumn day; a young lady had paused in her afternoon walk to lean on the parapet of a bridge across a pretty stream called the Gardenholme Linn. As she stared at the narrow, rocky stream, she noticed some kind of bundle that had jammed against a boulder. Something that looked unpleasantly like a human arm was sticking out of it.

The police were on the scene by mid-afternoon, and had soon discovered two human heads on the bank of the Linn, as well as four bundles, each containing human remains – thigh bones, legs, pieces of flesh, and an armless torso. One piece of newspaper wrapped round two upper arms proved to be the *Sunday Graphic* for 15 September 1935.

When, the following day, Professor John Glaister — author of a classic *Medical Jurisprudence and Toxicology* — arrived with his colleague Dr Gilbert Millar, he quickly realized that this killing was not the work of some terrified amateur; he had taken care to cover his tracks. He had not only dismembered the bodies, but removed the skin from the heads, to make the faces unrecognizable, and cut off the fingertips to make fingerprint identification impossible. He had made only one mistake: instead of tossing the remains into the River Annan, a few hundred yards downstream, he had tossed them into its tributary, the Linn, which had been swollen with heavy rains at the time. If the rain had continued, the parcels would have ended up in the Solway Firth. But there were a few days of fine weather; the stream dwindled to its usual trickle, and the parcels caught in the rocks.

The remains were sent to the Anatomy Department of the University of Edinburgh, and there treated with ether to prevent further decomposition and destroy maggots; then they were "pickled" in a formalin solution. Glaister and Millar found themselves confronted with a human jigsaw puzzle of seventy pieces.

The first task was to sort the pieces into two separate bodies, and this was made easier by the fact that one was six inches shorter than the other. And when it was finally done, Glaister and his team found that they had one almost complete body, the taller one, and one body minus a trunk. There was also an item that caused much bafflement — an enormous single eye, which certainly did not belong to either of the bodies; by some odd chance, this eye, probably from an animal, had also found its way into the Linn.

What could be deduced about the murderer? First, that he was almost certainly a medical man. He had used a knife, not a saw, to dismember the body, and a human body is almost impossible to dismember with a knife without detailed knowledge of the joints. He had also removed the teeth, recognizing that they could lead to identification by a dentist.

Fortunately, the murderer had either lost his nerve or been interrupted, for he had left some of the hair on the smaller body – which, at first, Glaister thought to be that of a man. And when more parcels were found in the river, Glaister found that he had a pair of hands that still had fingertips. After soaking them in hot water, he was able to get an excellent set of fingerprints. And the discovery that the assorted pieces of flesh included three breasts also made it clear that both bodies were of women.

The next problem was the age of the bodies. Glaister determined this by means of the skull sutures. Sutures are "joining lines" in the skull, and they seal themselves over the years; they are usually closed completely by the age of forty. In one of the two skulls, the smaller of the two, the sutures were unclosed; in the other, they were almost closed. This indicated that one body was that of a woman of about forty; the other was certainly under thirty. X-rays of the jaw-bone of the younger woman showed that the wisdom teeth had still not pushed through, which meant she was probably in her early twenties. The cartilage, the soft material of which bones are originally made, gradually changes into "caps", called "epiphyses", and the age can also be estimated from how far this change has taken place. The epiphyses of the smaller body confirmed that this was a girl of twenty or so; the other was of a woman approaching middle-age.

As to the cause of death, this was fairly clear. The taller woman had five stab wounds in the chest, several broken bones, and many bruises. The hyoid bone in the neck was broken, indicating strangulation before the other injuries had been inflicted. The swollen and bruised tongue confirmed this inference. Glaister reasoned that a murderer who strangled and beat his victim before stabbing her would probably be in the grip of jealous rage. As to the other body, the signs were that she had been battered with some blunt instrument. It hardly needed a Sherlock Holmes to infer that she had been killed as an afterthought, probably to keep her silent. The fact that the murderer had taken less trouble to conceal her identity pointed to the same conclusion.

Meanwhile, the police were working on their own clues. The *Sunday Graphic* was a special local edition, printed for the Morecambe and Lancaster area. And the clothes in which some of the remains had been wrapped were also distinctive: the head of the younger woman had been wrapped in a pair of child's rompers, and another bundle had been wrapped in a blouse with a patch under the arm . . .

And in Lancaster, a Persian doctor named Buck Ruxton had already attracted the suspicions of the local police. Five days before the remains were found in the Linn, Ruxton — a small, rather good-looking man with a wildly excitable manner — had called on the police and mentioned that his wife had deserted him. The police were investigating the murder of a lady called Mrs Smalley, whose body had been found a year earlier, and in the course of routine investigations, had questioned a domestic in Ruxton's household; he wanted to protest about this harassment. And when he spoke of his wife's disappearance, they were not in the least surprised; they knew that the relations between the two were stormy. Two years before, Mrs Isabella Ruxton had come to the police station to protest that her husband was beating her, and Ruxton had made wild accusations of infidelity against her; however, he had calmed down, and twenty-four hours later the two were apparently again on the best of terms.

The parents of Mrs Ruxton's maid, Mary Rogerson, were not only surprised but incredulous when Ruxton came and told them that their daughter had got herself pregnant by the laundry boy, and that his wife had taken her away for an abortion. Nothing was less likely; Mary was a plain girl, with a cast in one eye, who loved her home and her parents, and spent all her spare time with them; she was as unlikely to get herself pregnant as to rob a bank. In spite of Ruxton's feverish protests, they reported it to the police. On the evening of 9 October 1935, ten days after the remains had been found in the Linn, Ruxton came to the police and burst into tears. People were saying that he had murdered his wife and thrown her into the Linn; they must help him find her. They soothed him and sent him away. But, in fact, Ruxton had been the chief suspect since earlier that day. The Scottish police had been to see the Rogersons, and had shown them the patched blouse. As soon as they saw it, they knew their daughter was dead; Mary had bought it at a jumble sale and patched it under the arm. They were unable to identify the rompers, but suggested that the police show them to Mrs Holme, with whom Mary and the three Ruxton children had spent a holiday earlier that year. And Mrs Holme recognized the rompers as a pair she had given to Mary for the children.

The police spoke to the Ruxton's charlady, Mrs Oxley. She told them that on the day Mrs Ruxton and Mary Rogerson had disappeared, Sunday 15 September 1935, Ruxton had arrived early at her house and explained that it was unnecessary for her to come to work that day – he was taking the children to Morecambe, and his wife had gone to Edinburgh. The following morning, she found the Ruxton's house – at 2 Dalton Square – in a state of chaos, with carpets removed, the bath full of yellow stains, and a pile of burnt material in the yard. A neighbour told the police that Ruxton had persuaded her to come and clean up his house to prepare it for the decorators, claiming that he had cut his hand badly on a tin of peaches. She and her husband had obligingly scrubbed out the house. And Ruxton had given them some bloodstained carpets and a blue suit that was also stained with blood.

On 12 October, the police questioned Ruxton all night, and at 7.20 the next morning he was charged with the murder of Mary Rogerson.

In spite of Ruxton's attempts to cover his tracks, and to persuade various witnesses to offer him false alibis, the truth about the murders soon became plain. Ruxton was pathologically jealous, although there was no evidence that his "wife" — they were in fact unmarried — had ever been unfaithful. A week before the murder, Mrs Ruxton had gone to Edinburgh, where she had a sister, with a family named Edmondson, who were close friends of the Ruxtons. The Edmondsons and Mrs Ruxton had all booked into separate rooms; nevertheless, Ruxton was convinced that she had spent the night in the bed of Robert Edmondson, an assistant solicitor in the Town Hall. Ruxton had driven to Edinburgh to spy on them. The following Saturday, Isabella Ruxton had gone to spend the afternoon and evening with two of her sisters in Blackpool. Convinced that she was in a hotel room with a man, Ruxton had worked himself into a jealous frenzy, and when she came back far later than expected, he began to beat her — probably in an attempt to make her confess her infidelities — then throttled her unconscious and stabbed her. Mary Rogerson had probably heard the screams and come in to see what was happening; Ruxton believed she was his wife's confidant in her infidelities, and killed her too. He had spent the next day dismembering the bodies and packing them in straw; that night, he made his first trip north to dispose of the bodies . . .

Ruxton's counsel, Norman Birkett, must have known that his client did not stand a ghost of a chance. His line of defence was that the bodies found in the Linn were not those of Isabella Ruxton and Mary Rogerson, but of some other persons. But when the medical experts — Glaister, Millar, and Professor Sydney Smith — gave their evidence, it was obvious that the identity of the bodies had been established beyond all possible doubt. One photograph, which has subsequently been used in every account of the case, superimposed the larger of the two skulls on a photograph of Mrs Ruxton. She had a rather long, horsy face, and it was obvious that the two fitted together with gruesome exactitude. Ruxton seemed determined to trap himself in a web of lies and evasions. The result was a unanimous verdict of guilty, arrived at in only one hour. He was hanged at Strangeways jail, Manchester, on 12 May 1936.

Yet examination of the evidence — and of Glaister's famous book *Medico–legal Aspects of the Ruxton Case* (1937) — makes it clear that Ruxton came very close indeed to getting away with murder. If he had taken the trouble to remove Mary Rogerson's fingertips, and destroyed the telltale breast tissue as well as the trunk (which was never found), the evidence against him would have remained purely circumstantial; and since British juries are unwilling to convict on circumstantial evidence, he might well have been given the benefit of the doubt. Glaister's forensic skill and Ruxton's failure of nerve played an equal part in bringing him to the gallows.

Chapter Six

Cold-Blooded
Crimes of Passion

W hat brings a person to commit murder — high emotion,
unrequited love, monetary gain? Certainly in the case of
Albert Guay, who had a bomb planted on a plane, which not
only killed his wife but twenty-two other people as well; or when
you kill someone that you don't really even love, as in the case of
Ruth Ellis, just because they were refusing to speak to you, the
answer is sheer cold-bloodedness. The reasoning behind these sort
of crimes of passion surely cannot be explained in any other terms.

The Guay Case

I f there was a prize for the most cold-blooded of all
crimes of passion, it would probably go to Albert Guay.
On 9 September, 1949, a Quebec Airways Dakota DC-3
on a flight from Montreal to Seven Islands exploded in mid-
air, only minutes after take-off. The plane dived into
inaccessible forest near Sault-au-Cochon, forty miles north-
east of Quebec. All twenty-three passengers were killed.
Since witnesses noticed that the engines were still running
as it crashed, engine failure was clearly not the cause of the
disaster. But there was scorched metal in the luggage
compartment, suggesting an explosion. Chemical analysis
revealed minute traces of dynamite.

A careful check of every item of freight against the
company's list revealed that only one seemed to be missing,

a "religious statuette" weighing twenty-six pounds. But there was no record of its sender; all the reception could remember about the person who delivered it was that it was a woman dressed in black. An appeal through the news media failed to trace her. But ten days later, a taxi driver came forward to say that he had picked up a woman of this description on the day of the explosion. And he could also remember the address from which he had picked her up. This proved to be the home of a woman named Marie Pitre. But when the police tried to call on her, they learned that she was in hospital, recovering from the effects of an overdose of sleeping tablets.

As soon as she was able to give an interview, Marie Pitre told them how she had come to take the parcel to the airport. For many years she had been the mistress of a Quebec jeweller named Joseph Albert Guay, who was married. He had, she said, virtually blackmailed her into taking the statue to the airport by offering to cancel some of her promissory notes that he held. Their love affair had been over ever since he met an attractive nineteen year old night club cigarette girl named Marie-Ange Robitaille, who preferred to be called Mary Angel.

Then Marie Pitre dropped her bombshell. "I didn't know his wife would be on that flight." And she went on to describe how, some weeks before, Guay had telephoned her and asked her to purchase ten pounds of dynamite, which he needed for landscape gardening.

Assuming that it was this dynamite that had blown up the Dakota, how had it been detonated? It would need a timing mechanism. And Marie, they discovered, had a brother named Genereux Ruest who was an expert clock repairer . . . In fact, Ruest, who was a cripple, admitted that he had made the timing mechanism; Guay, he said, had told him that he needed it for exploding the dynamite to blow some rocks out of the ground.

Albert Guay, a thin-faced man with a pencil-line moustache, was arrested, and the newspapers headlined the "love bomb murder" — since it was by now plain that he had decided to kill his wife Rita in order to marry the pretty waitress Mary Angel. The crime caused such indignation that police had to hold back crowds who wanted to lynch the jeweller on the spot.

At the trial, Guay's defence lawyer had an impossible task; he was found guilty and sentenced to death. He met the hangman on 10 January, 1951. Eighteen months later, Marie Pitre and her brother also went to the gallows — new evidence had revealed that they had willingly participated in the murder plot that had killed twenty-two other people besides the intended victim.

Ruth Ellis

On the evening of Easter Sunday, 10 April, 1955, two men emerged from the Magdala public house in Hampstead, and walked towards the grey-green Vanguard parked outside. They were David Blakely, twenty-five, the manager of a small engineering firm in Penn, and a car salesman, Clive Gunnell, thirty. Both were carrying quarts of light ale, for they were about to return to a party which they had left to buy more beer. As Blakely fumbled for his keys, a small peroxide blonde woman approached him, calling out: "David." Blakely failed to hear her. Moments later she stood beside him, took a revolver from her handbag, and pointed it at him. Blakely gave a cry of alarm and ran towards the back of the car. Two shots hit him in the back. He started to run uphill, and another shot hit him. Even as he lay on the pavement, with Clive Gunnell bending over him, the woman went on firing over Gunnell's shoulder; one shot hit a female pedestrian in the thumb. When the hammer clicked on an empty chamber, the woman turned and said unemotionally: "Go and call the police." A man strode out of the pub. "I *am* a police officer." He took the revolver away from her. David Blakely was dead when the ambulance arrived.

The killer was twenty-eight-year-old Ruth Ellis, and she and David Blakely had been lovers for two years, ever since they met at a London club. Blakely was something of a playboy; he had a well paid job, an inheritance of £7,000 (a considerable sum in 1953) and an allowance from his stepfather. His passion in life was racing cars.

Their relationship had been stormy; both were inclined to be jealous and possessive. Both were also emotionally unstable. Ruth hungered for constant flattery and attention; Blakely was immature, and inclined to become so rude when drunk that he drove away many regular customers at the Little Club, of which Ruth was the manageress. Eventually, the proprietor fired Ruth, largely because of her relationship with Blakely. A businessman named Desmond Cussen took her – and her two small children – into his flat in Devonshire Place and financed her; he was so devoted to her that he even allowed her to continue to sleep with Blakely.

Ruth's intensely possessive attitude to Blakely was due partly to insecurity. Born into a relatively poor family in Rhyl, North Wales, (her father was a musician), Ruth Neilson had left school at fifteen and worked as a machinist in a factory and a Woolworth's shopgirl. At seventeen she had become a photographer's assistant, and soon fell in love with a French Canadian soldier named Clare. She learned she was pregnant soon after Christmas 1944. Clare had promised to marry her, but a letter to his C.O. revealed that he already had a wife and children in Canada. Ruth got herself a job as a cashier, and a daughter was born in 1944. Clare paid maintainence, but it stopped when he returned to Canada.

She became a photographer's model and often posed in the nude. In a Mayfair club she met vice-boss Morris

Conley, who was soon sleeping with her, and persuaded her to work for him as a hostess in the Court Club. She did not *have* to sleep with customers, but it helped her take-home pay. In 1950 she became pregnant again; she had an abortion. In November that year she married a recently divorced dentist, George Ellis — another customer — who was an alcoholic. He was forty-one, she twenty-four. A daughter was born in 1951, but by then her husband's alcoholism had been intensified by endless quarrels, often ending in violence, and they separated. She returned to being a club hostess for Maurice Conley, and in 1953, he made her manageress of the Little Club in Brompton Road, Knightsbridge. She received £25 a week and a rent-free flat. One client gave her £400 for going on holiday with him.

Her first meeting with the weakly handsome David Blakely was not a success — she remarked afterwards "I hope I never see that little shit again." But although Ruth had a violent temper she knew — as a hostess — how to keep it. Blakely had just become engaged to an heiress, but he was an incorrigible philanderer. Since Ruth made a habit of being available to customers of her choice, it was not too difficult to persuade her to let him sleep with her. He understood that he was not her "lover" — merely a customer who was being allowed to spend nights in her bed, as many others did. And, according to Ruth Ellis, she was not particularly in love with him either. Nevertheless, they seem to have found one another exciting in bed, and Blakely was soon sleeping in her flat five nights a week. They became lovers almost as a matter of habit. It was also a matter of vanity; Ruth liked the idea of having an affair with this ex-public schoolboy with his private income and racing car, and he liked the idea of having a sexy blonde mistress whose bed was right above the club.

In February 1954, she had an abortion — this time Blakely's baby. But while Blakely was away racing at Le Mans, she slept with her devoted admirer, Desmond

Cussen. He lent her money – she was insatiable where cash was concerned – and pressed her to marry him. Ruth was not interested – not because she preferred Blakely, for both of them slept with other people, but because she was not deeply attracted to Cussen. She may also have preferred Cussen as an adoring swain rather than a husband who might take her for granted. Cussen even arranged to send her son Andy to a private school.

Ruth and Blakely quarrelled after she noticed love-scratches on his back. He was the one who made it up, and the affair continued. Both of them were now drinking much more heavily. He often hit her when he lost his temper, on one occasion knocking her down the stairs. One night, she went back home with a man who had picked her up, and took off all her clothes to reveal bruises all over her body. Profits at the Club were sagging, and when Conley finally fired her at the end of 1954, she moved in with Desmond Cussen. But she often spent the night in a hotel with Blakely.

It was clear to their friends that the couple were bad for one another. Blakely was aggressive when drunk, and he was drunk much of the time. Ruth was less aggressive but gave as good as she got. They often quarrelled, but always made up in bed. Even when she knew he was having an affair with a married woman in Penn, she continued to let him sleep with her. Towards the end of January 1955, they went on a nine day drinking spree that ended with quarrels and hysteria. On another occasion Ruth hid his car keys, and when Clive Gunnell and another friend arrived to pick him up, Ruth had a black eye and many bruises. There was another hysterical scene when Blakely found his car keys and tried to drive off. Yet after more bitter recriminations, he sent her red carnations with a note: "Sorry darling. I love you. David." When she decided to leave Cussen's flat, the faithful admirer lent her the money to rent a new one in Kensington. When Blakely told her he had broken off his affair with the married woman, she allowed him to stay there with her. She then persuaded Cussen to take her down to a pub in Penn, and found Blakely in there with the woman. Back in Kensington, after another violent quarrel, he hit her in the stomach and caused a miscarriage.

In spite of this, they spent the night before Good Friday, 1955, in her flat. Ruth had become extremely sexually demanding, and Blakely was taking amyl nitrite, a sexual stimulant. He left the flat early because he found her son Andy (now ten) too noisy. Later that day he told friends – a married couple named Findlater – that he couldn't stand it any longer, and had to get away from her. Carole Findlater, who had once been Blakely's girlfriend, was glad to hear it; she disliked Ruth intensely. She persuaded Blakely to come home for lunch, and that night he stood Ruth up and went out with them. Late at night, Ruth repeatedly rang the Findlaters demanding to talk to him. When they refused – or hung up when they recognized her voice – she drove around to their flat and smashed in all the windows of Blakely's car. The police arrived, and Ruth was finally driven back home by Desmond Cussen.

The following day – Saturday – was spent unsuccessfully pursuing Blakely – Ruth was now convinced he was making love to the nursemaid of the Findlaters. Until late that night she hung around opposite the Findlaters' flat. She went home in the early hours of the morning, and telephoned the Findlaters; again she failed to speak to Blakely.

On Sunday, there was another party at the Findlaters, after a lunchtime drink at the Magdala public house. At 9 that evening, Carole Findlater ran out of cigarettes, and asked Blakely to go and get her some. Blakely decided they also needed more beer, and asked Clive Gunnell to go with him to the Magdala public house . . .

According to Ruth Ellis – speaking shortly before her execution – she had been pouring out her fury to Desmond Cussen when he had handed her a loaded revolver. He had then driven her to woodland where she practised shooting. And later, she alleged, he drove her to the Magdala public house. She arrived minutes before David Blakely came out with Clive Gunnel. Soon after that, David Blakely lay dead on the pavement, and Ruth Ellis was taken into custody.

On Monday 20 June, 1955, Ruth Ellis stood in the dock at the Old Bailey. And when she told the prosecuting Q.C, Christmas Humphreys, that she had intended to kill Blakely, the judge warned the jury that only one verdict was possible: murder. They took only fourteen minutes to arrive at the guilty verdict.

The campaign for the abolition of capital punishment was then in full swing, and many petitions for her reprieve were sent to the Home Secretary, one with 50,000 signatures. But the bank manager's wife who had been wounded in the hand by Ruth Ellis, wrote a letter to a newspaper pointing out that if Ruth was reprieved, "other vindictive and jealous young women" might begin gunning down their boyfriends. She had actually witnessed the murder, and obviously felt that a woman who could shoot someone with such deliberate intent deserved to die.

The knowledge that her reprieve had been turned down did not seem to bother Ruth Ellis; she wrote to one friend that being hanged would be no worse than having a tooth out. On 13 July, 1955, she drank a hot brandy, then walked firmly the few steps to the execution shed. She was the last woman to be hanged in England – ten years later, in 1965, capital punishment was abolished.

Clive Gunnell had a nervous breakdown after witnessing his friend being shot at close range. He told the present author that he rejected the idea that Ruth killed David Blakely because she was so much in love with him. He felt she was an exhibitionist who wanted to "become known", and that the murder was a theatrical performance as much as a *crime passionel*. Years of drunken parties and prostitution (for she was basically a high class call girl) had led to states of depression and boredom when she needed emotional stimulants. She killed Blakely because she was infuriated at his refusal to speak to her or see her after their last lovemaking session on Good Friday; there may also have been an element of self-disgust in her decision to make the break final by killing him. Her death, Gunnell argued, was a spectacular form of suicide.

The De Kaplany Case

What is the most horrific crime of passion on record? There is a body of opinion in favour of a French case of 1958, which the press labelled "the demon lovers". Dr Yves Evenou was to all appearances a happily married man, who sometimes referred to his wife, Marie-Claire as an angel. But Evenou harboured peculiar sexual tastes of which his wife knew nothing. In 1953, when a dressmaker named Simone Deschamps came to his surgery, Evenou divined instantly that this rather plain forty-three year old woman was a masochist, and therefore his ideal sex partner. They became lovers, and she submitted to sexual demands that included flagellation and semi-public strip-tease. In 1958, Evenou decided his wife had to die, and that the crime should be performed by his mistress — in the nude. By now, Simone Deschamps had moved into a flat directly underneath that occupied by the Evenous. On the evening of the murder, Evenou telephoned her, and she mounted the stairs wearing only a coat and shoes. In his flat she removed these. He then led her to the bed where his wife — a semi-invalid — lay half drugged. Evenou pulled back the bedclothes and ordered his mistress to strike. But Simone's hands were weak, and the first blow only awakened Marie-Claire. Evenou held her down while Simone completed the butchery, stabbing her eleven

The Denise Labbé case is perhaps one of the most sinister crimes of passion on record. Twenty-year-old Denise, a secretary, enjoyed mixing – and sleeping – with students at Rennes, and had a baby daughter, Catherine, by one of them. Then she met officer cadet, Jacques Algarron, a brilliant mathematician who believed ardently in Nietzsche's theory of the superman. He decided that he and Denise were a "super-couple", and that to prove that she was above conventional morality, she should kill her daughter. She was so besotted with him that she agreed. Delays brought threats to break off the affair. Eventually, she tried to throw Catherine from a high window, but found she could not bring herself to do it. Then she pushed her into the canal, but relented, and summoned help. A second attempt at drowning was frustrated when neighbours heard the child's cries and pulled her out of the river. On 8 November, 1954, Denise Labbé finally drowned Catherine in a stone wash basin. Friends were suspicious, and Denise was questioned by police. Finally, she confessed, implicating her lover. "It was a ritual murder". She was sentenced to life imprisonment, Algarron to twenty years hard labour.

times. The murder of Marie-Claire Evenou was less an attempt to dispose of an unwanted wife than an act of sexual perversion by two lovers who had tried everything.

There was hardly any attempt to cover up the crime, and the lovers were arrested almost immediately. Evenou died before the trial – a life of excess had drained his vitality. Simone Deschamps escaped the death penalty, but received life imprisonment with hard labour.

But even the crime of Simone Deschamps sounds humane in comparison with the murder committed by the Hungarian doctor, Geza de Kaplany. He had fled from communist persecution in Hungary, and took up practice in San Jose, California, in 1962, as an anaesthesiologist in a hospital. Kaplany was good looking in a cold, thin-lipped way. He soon fell violently in love with a beauty queen who was more than ten years his junior, and married her in 1962. But only a few days after he and Hajna moved into their apartment, he became impotent with his wife. He convinced himself that all the men in the apartment building were pursuing her, and that she was encouraging them. This, at all events, is the excuse he gave for what followed.

Kaplany bought himself a record player, and on the morning of 28 August, 1962, neighbours became indignant at the tremendous volume at which Kaplany was playing his new toy. They could also hear a woman's piercing screams above the music. Finally, the police arrived, and pounded on the door until it opened. Kaplany stood there in bloodstained underwear, and wearing rubber gloves. On the bed lay Hajna de Kaplany, so mutilated that the police were sickened. Kaplany had tied her hands and feet to the bedposts, then made razor cuts all over her body, into which he poured hydrochloric, sulphuric and nitric acid. He mutilated her face, her genitals, her breasts. His aim, he explained later, was not to kill her but to make sure that she ceased to be attractive to males.

Hajna died twenty-four hours later in hospital, while her mother knelt beside the bed and prayed – not for her to live, but to die.

At the trial, Kaplany became hysterical as he viewed the photographs of his wife's mutilated body. He was found guilty and sentenced to life imprisonment.

Crimes of Passion

In fact, Kaplany was released after only eleven years, even before he was due for parole. Then he was virtually smuggled out of the country, to take up duties in Taiwan as a "cardiac specialist" — a position for which he was unqualified. The parole board never explained its strange decision — it may have been due to the feeling that his life would have been in danger if he had been released in the normal way.

This seems highly probable, since his crime was probably the most sadistic in American criminal history.

Chapter Seven

Late 20th-Century Crimes of Passion

E.ven in the late twentieth century crimes of passion still occur, with the methods of murder similar to those used in the early twentieth century, or even back to the eighteenth century. The methods used being a gun, knife, or bludgeon. Even in this knowledgable and relaxed age (as opposed to the Victorian era), people are still overtaken by emotions that they cannot control and that cause them to murder.

The Red Mini Murder

At about 10 p.m. Thursday 2 March, 1967, a red Morris Mini crashed into a beech tree at Rummerhedge Wood, near Henley-on-Thames, west of London. Police Constable Sherlock arrived in his patrol car, to find three men at the scene of the accident. They explained that the two victims of the crash had already been taken to hospital by ambulance — an unconscious woman and a dazed man. They were merely witnesses who had arrived after the crash. One of them explained that when they had arrived, a man had already been there, bending over the woman, who was stretched out on the ground. The man had told them that he was going to his car to get a blanket — the witnesses had passed a dark Cortina parked around the bend — but a few moments later, they heard him drive off.

Sherlock decided that the accident could not have been serious, since the car was not badly damaged, and the windscreen was unbroken. But he noted the large quantity of blood on the driver's side, and inferred that the driver had been badly cut.

PC Sherlock went home, and telephoned the Battle Hospital in Reading — to learn, to his surprise, that the woman, a Mrs June Serina Cook, was dead. He immediately drove to the hospital and saw the dead woman. June Cook's head was bandaged, and the surgeon explained that she had severe head injuries, and that he had had to perform a tracheotomy to allow her to breathe.

Sherlock also interviewed Raymond Sidney Cook, the husband of the dead woman, who had been in the car with her. He smelt of alcohol and seemed to be in shock. His replies to questions were incoherent mumbles. But he accepted Sherlock's offer to drive him home — to Spencer's Wood, near Reading — and Sherlock was surprised that he was able to give precise instructions about the route, although he relapsed into mumbles when asked about the accident.

The Cooks had apparently lived next door to June Cook's parents, and Sherlock also went to interview them. He learned that June Cook was a schoolteacher who was nine years older than her thirty-two-year-old husband. June's parents had given them the house next door. But they seemed to disapprove of their son-in-law, and told Sherlock that the Cooks had been quarrelling recently.

Next, the indefatigable Sherlock went back and looked again at the scene of the accident. He had already noticed that there were no skid marks. Yet there were pieces of bark on the ground which the Mini had knocked off the tree. Had it been driven into the tree fairly slowly, to give the impression of an accident? He had noted earlier that when he had reversed the car, there was no need to adjust the rear view mirror. Yet the dead woman was six inches shorter than he was, and it was her blood that stained the driver's seat . . .

The next day Sherlock went to look at the Mini in the garage to which it had been towed. It had now been cleaned out, but he noticed there were bloodstains *on the outside* of the car. It was just possible that they had got there when the ambulance men moved the body. But why was there also hair soaked in blood near the *rear* wheel?

He talked again to Cook, who was now able to describe how, as his wife was driving, a car had dazzled them with its headlights. The next thing he knew was waking up dazed . . .

Sherlock had requested the aid of a Scene of Crimes officer, and when Sergeant McMiken arrived, he took him to Rummerhedge Wood. As he was setting up his camera, McMiken noticed something that had escaped Sherlock – a dark stain on the road seventy five yards from the scene of the accident; it looked like dried blood. All this made it clear that Cook's story of the accident could not be true.

The pathologist who examined Mrs Cook's body agreed when he was told that the windscreen was undamaged; he had assumed – from her broken neck – that she had been thrown through the windscreen. He also noted that Mrs Cook's bloodstream indicated that, like her husband, she had been drinking heavily. This was confirmed by Raymond Cook, who was now well enough to elaborate his story (although he still spoke very slowly, as if weighing every word). He explained that he and his wife always went out for dinner on a Thursday. On this particular evening, both had drunk a large amount at the George Hotel in Pangbourne. On the way home, he had felt faint, and his wife had taken over the driving. Soon after that, the oncoming car had dazzled them both . . .

But June Cook's parents were able to add an interesting piece of information to the jigsaw puzzle. Raymond Cook had been having an affair with a young blonde named Kim

— they thought her surname was Mule — a nurse at the Borocourt Mental Hospital.

Detective Inspector Insel, who now took charge of the investigation, decided that the most important question was the identity of the man who had driven off in the dark Cortina. Luck was on his side. When newspapers published the story, a house painter named Angus Macdonald came forward to say that he had seen the Cortina on the evening of the accident. He did not know the identity of the male driver, but he *did* happen to know the identity of the attractive blonde who was in the car with him. It was Kim Newell, Raymond Cook's girlfriend, who happened to live next door to MacDonald's mother. MacDonald had even been curious enough to take the car's number — 7711 FM.

This was a major stroke of luck. The Cortina proved to belong to a heavy plant hire company in Wrexham, and when the police arrived, a man named Eric Jones was just getting into the car. Jones insisted that he had been nowhere near Reading or Rummerhedge Wood on 2 March, and gave an elaborate alibi. The police appeared to accept this; but their investigation into Jones's background revealed that he had also had an affair with Kim Newell before she met Raymond Cook. At a second interview, Jones changed his story about being nowhere near Reading on the day of the accident; he now admitted that he had been to see Kim Newell; she wanted to consult him about an abortion.

The father of the unborn child, apparently, was Raymond Cook. And Cook's background made it clear that he had a motive for killing his wife. She held the purse strings, and had some £10,000 in the bank, as well as owning various properties that provided an income in rent. At one point, Cook had left her to go and live with Kim Newell, and his wife had changed her will, leaving her money to the children, and also cancelled their joint bank account, containing £3,000. She had told the local vicar that her husband had agreed to return to her if she made some financial provision for him. And he had, in fact, returned in January 1967, two months before the accident.

The Home Office pathologist who examined Mrs Cook's body suggested that her neck had been broken by a heavy blow while she was kneeling on the ground, possibly with a second person holding her head.

On 17 March, the police felt they had enough evidence to charge Cook with his wife's murder. Soon after that, some new and important information came to light. A local dairyman went to the police to report a conversation between his wife and Kim's sister Janett; Kim Newell had told her sister that Eric Jones had murdered June Cook with a car jack. Her motive in making this disclosure was that she was afraid that Jones might also kill her, since she knew the truth . . .

A story of brutal and deliberate murder now emerged. Kim Newell had left her job, and was being supported by Raymond Cook. But Cook needed money; that was the only reason that he had returned to his wife. His solution to the problem of two "wives" was to plan the murder of the woman who held the purse strings – as soon as she had changed her will back in his favour. Eric Jones, Kim's ex-lover, had been drawn into the plot (although it is not clear what precisely he gained from his involvement in the murder). Their first plan involved driving the car into the river, but that was abandoned. On the night of the murder, Cook had been delayed – he was supposed to show Jones the site chosen for the murder. Instead, Kim Newell had to do it.

Later that evening, as the Cooks drove back from dinner, Jones thumbed a lift, claiming that his car had broken down. From the back seat he struck June Cook – who was in the passenger seat – a violent blow on the head; but it only stunned her. She was dragged from the car and beaten to death with the car jack by Jones, while her husband held her head. Then the car was driven into the tree, and June was placed in the driver's seat.

The full story of the murder was told to the police by Kim Newell when she was arrested. As a result, she stood beside Raymond Cook and Eric Jones in the dock, although a charge of murder against her was dropped in favour of a charge of being an accessory before the fact. All three were sentenced to life imprisonment.

The Jean Harris Case

This book has so far contained no example of the commonest type of crime of passion – the murder of a husband (or lover) – by a rejected wife or mistress. In 1981, just such a case made headlines in America, and even in Europe; the reason was that the victim was something of a celebrity, and that the homicidal lady was also the highly respectable headmistress of an expensive girls' school in Virginia. The *New York Times* referred to the trial as "one of the most sensational ever".

Dr Herman Tarnower had become wealthy as a result of a simple invention, the "Scarsdale medical diet"; his book about it had been on the best-sellers lists for a long time. (Scarsdale is an expensive dormitory suburb of New York.) When Jean Harris met Dr Tarnower in 1966, she was forty-two; the doctor was fifty-six. The son of poor Jewish immigrants who had settled in Brooklyn, the intensely ambitious doctor had "played life to win". He had had a long succession of attractive blonde mistresses, and had ruthlessly terminated relationships when he was tired of them. He also ran the Scarsdale Medical Center, with the aid of his latest mistress, Lynne Tryforos, who, at thirty-seven, was twenty-two years his junior.

Jean Harris's life had also been a success story. She had majored in economics at the exclusive Smith College for girls, married a childhood sweetheart at twenty-three, and separated from him nineteen years later when she felt she had outgrown him. That was in 1965, a year before she met Tarnower. By then she had become an administrator in Springside School in Philadelphia.

She had been introduced to Tarnower at a dinner party, and these two highly intelligent people had found one another fascinating. Soon Tarnower was proposing marriage. In fact, he had never been married, and had just broken his promise to marry another woman. Jean Harris and "Hy" Tarnower travelled widely and often spent weekends together in the Hotel Pierre in New York. The idea of marriage was tactfully shelved, for she realized that he valued his freedom. In 1971 she improved her professional position by moving to Connecticut as headmistress of a private school, and in 1977, she moved again to the Madeira School in Virginia.

Even as early as 1972 she was aware that there were other women in Tarnower's life – in particular the twenty-nine year-old divorcee Lynne Tryforos, whose letters often followed them around the world. Mrs Harris regarded Lynne Tryforos as "a vicious adulteress and psychotic". But the adulteress had the advantage of being at Tarnower's side most of the time. In January 1980, Tarnower took Jean Harris to Miami for the New Year, but on New Year's Day, her holiday was spoiled when she saw a message in the personal column on front of the *New York Times*; it read: "Hy T. Love always. Lynne."

The week of 7 March, 1980, had been a time of emotional stress; she had decided to expel four seniors when drugs were found in the dormitory. After that, she wrote Tarnower a ten page letter, which she sent by recorded delivery – because he claimed that some of her previous letters had failed to reach him. One writer on the case has spoken of its "insults hurled at Lynne Tryforos, its paranoid obsession with financial minutiae and its pitiable, distasteful grovelling." It was the letter of a woman who hated herself for her weakness, and hated — as well as adored — her lover. After sending it — on 10 March — she finalized her will, then rang Tarnower to tell him she was driving from Virginia to his home in Westchester. "Suit yourself" he said resignedly. He did not realize that she had recently bought a .32 revolver.

That evening, Tarnower gave a dinner party at which Lynne Tryforos was one of the guests. There was a conversation about wives murdering their husbands, and Tarnower remarked: "That is one of the advantages of being a bachelor — that could never happen to me." The party was over by 9; the guests — including Lynne — departed, and Tarnower went to bed early, as was his wont.

Jean Harris arrived at 10.30, and went in through the garage. She almost certainly expected to find her rival in Tarnower's bed, and was prepared to kill them both. In fact, Tarnower was alone, and that should have defused her murderous intentions. Unfortunately, Tarnower had made a mistake that cost him his life — he had forgotten to conceal his other mistress's night clothes and hair curlers. As the light came on, Tarnower woke up and said: "Jesus Christ, Jean, it's the middle of the night." He watched resignedly as Jean Harris stormed around the bedroom and threw the nightgown and curlers out of the window. When she went into hysterics he applied the recognized remedy and slapped her face; she stopped screaming. But the sight of the nightclothes had revived her jealous fury; she opened her handbag and took out the gun. As Tarnower grabbed it, it went off and shattered his hand. Still holding the gun, Tarnower picked up the telephone and pressed the button that would connect him with his housekeepers, the van der Vrekens. That was his second mistake — he should have thrown the gun out of the window first. Jean Harris lunged for it, and as they struggled, she pulled the trigger three times. Tarnower slumped between the twin beds, dying.

When a police patrolman arrived minutes later, summoned by the van der Vrekens, he saw a car with Virginia license plates making a U-turn. As he jumped out, a woman in a bloodstained white blouse told him: "Someone's been shot." She then went back into the house, and followed the patrolman up to the bedroom. As the patrolman tried to revive the dying man, Jean Harris sat on one of the twin beds and asked: "Hy, why didn't you kill me?"

Her story was that she had driven up to Westchester intending to kill herself – in fact, she had placed the gun to her head before Tarnower wrested it from her. When she had asked him to kill her, he had said: "Get out of here, you're crazy!" The gun had gone off accidentally as they struggled, then jammed. But even after Tarnower had collapsed, she had tried to kill herself – she went into the bathroom and banged it on the bath to try to unjam it.

Jean Harris was arrested and fingerprinted, then taken to court in White Plains. There she was granted bail. Instead of returning to Virginia, she then admitted herself to a local hospital "for rest and recuperation".

Tarnower's death gave his book a new lease of life; to the delight of his publishers, *The Scarsdale Medical Diet* rocketed up the best-seller charts.

Jean Harris's defence at her trial – which began on 21 November before Judge Russell B. Leggett – was that her only intention in going to see Tarnower was to commit suicide. But the fact that Tarnower had been shot four times undermined her insistence that the gun had gone off accidentally in the course of the struggle. And if she had intended to give herself up, as she alleged, why had she tried to escape, and only made a U-turn when she saw the police car with its flashing red light? It seemed clear that she was hoping to escape unrecognized, and that she only changed her mind and decided to "come clean" when she saw there was no hope of keeping her presence a secret. It seemed equally obvious that she had then decided on the suicide defence.

Jurors were impressed by her calm, quiet demeanour. But all that changed as they listened to the letter she had sent to her lover by recorded delivery, with its hysterical accusations. It made it very plain that she had gone to see Tarnower with murder in mind. Jean Harris was clearly a highly controlled woman who would tell whatever lies might influence the jury. In fact, it took the jury eight days to reach their verdict. But on 29 March, 1981, she was sentenced to fifteen years to life – a verdict that means that she could have no hope of parole before 1996.

The evidence presented in court made it clear that Tarnower was a lifelong seducer who took pleasure in having mistresses shuttling in and out of his bed – he is quoted as saying: "I don't love anyone and I don't need anyone" – and that he had undoubtedly treated Jean Harris very badly indeed. But the guilty verdict was a proof that her plea of being under intolerable emotional pressure failed to convince a jury who recognized her as a highly controlled woman who killed out of a desire for revenge.

The Pam Smart Case

In March 1991, a murder case involving a pretty twenty-three-year-old widow created the same kind of sensation as the Jean Harris trial ten years earlier. Pam Smart was accused of persuading her sixteen-year-old schoolboy lover to murder her husband so that she could claim his insurance money and – sooner or later – marry her lover.

Pamela Wojas was born in Miami, Florida, in August 1967. In 1980, alarmed by Miami's soaring crime rate, the Wojases moved to Windham, New Hampshire. Her father was an airport worker who had worked his way up to airline pilot. As a highschool student, Pam (or Pame, as she preferred to spell it) got herself noticed a great deal as a girl who liked to be noticed. She also acquired a reputation for promiscuity, and the nickname "Seka", which referred to a pornographic movie star.

On New Year's Eve 1985, Pam attended a party at the home of a young man called Greg Smart, who had a reputation as the local stud – at one party, he was said to have "scored" with three girls in the course of the evening, none of them knowing about the others. These two intensely egotistical young people saw one another as a natural challenge; but Pam was the more smitten of the two. When Pam returned to the University of Florida, in Tallahassee, Greg seemed to have no regrets at seeing her go. But during the summer vacation, they saw a great deal of one another. And in 1987, Greg startled his friends by announcing that he was moving to Florida to be near Pam. She found herself a job as a disc jockey with a small local radio station, and Greg helped her select the records. Soon they were living together. In January 1988, when Pam was twenty and Greg twenty-two, they decided to get married. It was then that Greg realized that he would need to find himself a good job if he intended to offer Pam the kind of middle class comforts to which they were both accustomed. He decided to become an insurance salesman; Pam hoped to be a TV reporter.

The problem was that two such dominant personalities were bound to quarrel. Pam was determined to "be on top"; Greg had no intention of letting her. When they were bickering one evening in a restaurant, he squirted a mouthfull of beer in her face. The bouncer threw him out, but eventually let him back on a promise of good behaviour. Ten minutes later, they began to bicker again, and he squirted more beer in her face. This time the bouncer threw him out for good.

Crimes of Passion

Back in New Hampshire, the Smarts moved into Summerhill Condominiums, in the small community of Derry, and Greg quickly became a promising insurance salesman, while Pam took a step towards realizing her TV ambitions by becoming the director of the media centre at School Administrative Unit 21 in Hampton. Her job was to "generate positive publicity". The couple married in May 1989. Their condominium cost $750 a month, and they ran two cars. In their first year of married life, Greg earned $42,000, and Pam more than $29,000. They dined often with Greg's parents, and went to a restaurant twice a week. Married life looked promising.

But they continued to have pesonality clashes. When Pam "bitched" too much, Greg was still inclined to squirt beer in her face, and on one occasion when he came in drunk in the early hours of the morning, she left him to go home to mother. But the quarrel was soon made up. At School Unit 21, Pam Smart had many admirers. One fifteen year old called Billy Flynn turned to a friend after she had been introduced to his class and murmured: "I'm in love." And another student, fifteen year old Cecelia Pierce, also developed a crush on the young publicity director. Both teenagers had a chance to get to know Pam better when they collaborated with her in a competition to make a video commercial to advertise the nutritive qualities of orange juice. Billy Flynn was the cameraman. He also devised some of the music — thumping electronic rap. Pam enjoyed being group leader, and she accepted Cecelia's adoration as casually as she accepted Billy's obvious devotion. Billy was not happy at home — his father, an alcoholic, had showed him little affection, but when he was killed in a crash caused by his drunkness, Billy was shattered.

Just before Christmas 1989 — when the Smarts had been married a little over six months — Greg came home at 6 a.m. claiming that he had spent the night at the home of a friend. He finally admitted that he had spent the night with another woman. Pam was outraged. She was also upset by Greg's heavy drinking — on one occasion she arrived at the home of her in-law's in her night dress, saying that Greg had tried to strangle her.

It was not in her nature to take this kind of thing lying down. The obvious revenge was infidelity. But with whom? Billy Flynn was the obvious choice. One day she asked him: "Do you ever think of me when I'm not around?" "Sure" said Billy. "I think of you all the time." Soon after this, they drove to Billy Flynn's house when no one else was home. They went up to his bedroom to play records, and Billy locked the door. "Aren't you going to kiss me?" asked Pam. "Yeah." "Or do I have to come over there and rape you?" Tentatively, they exchanged their first kiss. Pam seems to have felt instinctively that it was better to move slowly.

In mid-February 1989, when Greg was on a skiing holiday, Pam invited Billy and Cecelia to her condominum. After they had listened to records for a while, Pam and Billy went upstairs; he stripped naked, and she went into the bathroom and put on a filmy nightdress. She came out and danced for him, then the two had sex. Billy assured her that it was not his first experience, but it was untrue. After that they made love at every opportunity; on one occasion when they were both naked on the grass beside a parking lot, a car pulled in and they both had to make a run for it; Billy hurt his knee. On another occasion a man caught them having sex in the back of a car, and yelled indignantly.

It was also at about this time that Pam told Billy that if they were to be together forever, they would have to kill Greg. At first he thought it was a joke; but the persistence with which she returned to the idea made it clear that she was serious. Her plan was that Billy should go to their home and kill Greg while she was at a school meeting, to establish an alibi.

Oddly enough, Cecelia was also told about the plan. She pooh-poohed the idea. "He's never going to do it." Bill, she said, was too gentle by nature. She later explained that she did not take the plot seriously. But Pam was deadly serious – as Cecelia realized on 2 May, 1990 . . .

At about 10.20 on the previous evening, neighbours who lived near the Smart's condominium in Derry were electrified by a series of piercing screams. As they peered out of their windows they heard a woman call: "Help! My husband, my husband . . ." The neighbours next door preferred to lie low and ignored her as she banged on the door; it was a young married woman who lived two doors away who let her in. When two men finally looked into Pam Smart's house, they saw Greg Smart lying face down on the floor, with blood running from his nose. The police arrived soon after. It took them only moments to determine that Greg was dead. The post mortem revealed that he had been shot in the top of the head.

Pam seemed shattered; various neighbours tried to comfort her. But the detective who interviewed her that evening felt she seemed oddly calm for a woman who had just lost her newly wedded spouse. Friends were also inclined to wonder why she did not cry more. But they accepted Pam's suggestion that God was giving her the strength to bear the shock.

Apparently the murder had been committed by a burglar, or burglars. The house was in wild disarray. Greg's wallet was empty, but a diamond ring lay beneath him. Various items – such as a TV and video – had been placed near the doors as if for quick removal; it looked as if the burglars had been interrupted, or had simply panicked.

When marijuana was found in Greg Smart's pickup truck, neighbours evolved a new theory – that he had been killed by drug traffickers to whom he owed money. More than a month passed by with no leads. Then, in the second week of June, the whole case broke open.

On the evening of Saturday 9 June, a youth named Ralph Welch listened with incredulity as two of his closest friends,

Pete Randall and JR Lattime, described how, together with Billy Flynn, they had murdered Greg Smart. Ralph had heard rumours of the killing that afternoon from another youth. It seemed that the deal to murder Greg Smart had been discussed around the area for at least a month before it happened. Billy's affair with Pam was also common knowledge. In this small community, most of the boys had known one another since childhood, and secrets were seldom kept for long. When Ralph confronted JR and Pete with questions about the murder, they at first denied it, then told him the whole story. Ralph Welch was horrified, and told them that he could not keep silent. The three argued about it for a long time. The following day, more bickering turned to blows, after which Ralph went to JR's parents and told them that their son had been involved in the murder of Greg Smart, and that Billy Smart had killed Greg with a gun belonging to JR's father Vance.

Around midday on Sunday, Vance and Diane Lattime, dazed but determined to get to the truth, called at the police station and told them the whole story. Meanwhile, JR and Pete called on Billy Flynn, who had spent the night with Pam, and told him that all hell was about to break. Pam and her lover were incredulous that they could have been so stupid as to tell Ralph Welch about the murder. Later that day, the three boys fled in the car belonging to Pete's mother. "He's my kid", said Mrs Randall, "I'd do anything I could to help him." But the flight was of short duration. In Connecticut, they called on Pete Randall's grandparents and explained they were in trouble and had to lie low for a while. Pete's grandfather called Pete's father, and Pete was summarily ordered to return home or face arrest. So the boys climbed back into the car and drove back to Derry. The following day, they were arrested.

Pam Smart was reacting more calmly. She was certain that her lover would protect her, and she was right. But she was unaware that there was a weak link in the chain: Cecelia

Pierce. When the police heard rumours that Cecelia had known about the murder before it happened, they took her in for questioning. She flatly denied everything – until a detective told her firmly that if she was later proved to be lying, she would be charged with obstructing an investigation. Cecilia decided to cooperate. The plan the police suggested was that she should telephone Pam Smart, and try to get her to say something incriminating. And the conversation would be recorded . . .

But Pam was not ready to incriminate herself. When Cecilia rang her at work and asked if Pam wanted her to continue denying that she and Billy had been lovers, Pam replied: "But we weren't." "*What?*" "We weren't." But in subsequent conversations – the police made sure Cecelia persisted – she made a number of comments that later formed an important part of the case against her.

One of her problems was to let Billy and his friends know she was not abandoning them; she shocked and startled some of her friends by saying that she would like to visit her husband's killers in jail, because, after all, they were only kids. She also sent Billy's mother a tape of heavy metal music that Billy had assembled for her (including a song called "Hot for Teacher"), with a note asking her to pass it on to him. When the police came to question her – ostensibly because she had known the accused boys well – she tried to convince them that they were not guilty. She even repeated some of the remarks she had made on the telephone to Cecelia the day before, giving them a turn that underlined her innocence – and also making it clear that she suspected the phone had been tapped.

On Wednesday 1 August, 1990 – three months after the murder – Officer Dan Palletier called on Pam at work. "Well, Pam, I have some good news and some bad news. The good news is that we've solved the murder of your husband. The bad news is that you're under arrest."

Her indictment on a murder charge made headlines. The newspapers found the story of her affair with a fifteen-year-old irresistable. They were equally fascinated by rumours that Cecelia had provided the information that led to her arrest in a series of taped phone conversations. Pam Smart proved to have many friends, who attended the pre-trial hearings wearing yellow ribbons: ribbons normally worn as a reminder of hostages in the Middle East. These were worn, they said, for "our hostage in the state of New Hampshire."

On 22 January, 1991, Pam Smart's supporters were dealt a heavy blow. Pete Randall agreed to a deal with the prosecution in which he would testify against Pam in exchange for a more lenient sentence. JR and Billy Flynn decided to follow suit.

Jury selection began on 19 February. On 5 March, the prosecution began to tell the story of the murder. Later in the day, Pete Randall took the stand, and described in a flat voice how, on May, 1990, he had gone to pick up the car belonging to JR's grandmother, "in order to go to Derry to kill Greg Smart."

Three days later, Billy Flynn described, equally factually, how he had first kissed Pam, and how they had first made love. (Resulting headlines were: "Smart killer recounts sex romp" and "Teacher seduced me with striptease".) He went on to describe how he and the other two boys had driven up to the empty house, and entered by an unlocked door in the basement. When Greg Smart finally came home, Billy Flynn grabbed him and began to hit him; Pete Randall threatened Greg with a knife and made him get down on his knees. Greg asked about his dog, and was told it was safe. When Pete asked for the diamond wedding ring, Greg refused. "My wife would kill me." He pleaded for his life, and the boys were moved – so much so that Pete Randall, who was supposed to slit Greg Smart's throat, could no longer bring himself to do it; he signalled to Billy Flynn, who took his revolver out, held it a few inches above the kneeling man's skull. He described how he had said "God forgive me" before he squeezed the trigger. As Pete Randall let go of Greg Smart's hair, Smart slumped on to the carpet. As he described the scene, Billy Flynn cried uncontrollably.

When Cecelia Pierce took the stand, she described how she had walked into the bedroom and found Pam and Billy naked on the floor, with Pam on top. One reporter murmured: "Why doesn't that surprise me?" In fact, Cecelia's testimony proved less crucial than the state had originally hoped. It had emerged that she had agreed to help the boys find a gun to kill Greg Smart, which made her virtually an accomplice. Her testimony was therefore bound to be suspect. The evidence of the tapes nevertheless left most jurors with no doubt that Pam Smart was guilty.

When Pam Smart took the stand, she conceded that she and Billy Flynn had been lovers, although she gave the date of their first sex act as mid-March rather than mid-February; in that time, Billy Flynn had become sixteen, and Pam could not be charged with having sex with a minor. She also insisted that she had wanted to end the affair, and had done so a month before her husband's murder. But Billy had been in her home just before the break, and had been in the basement by himself. The implication was that he had left the door open so he could break in and murder Greg Smart.

As to the incriminating tape conversations, Pam explained that she had believed that Cecelia knew more about the murder than she was telling, and was simply trying to get her to confess by pretending to know more about it than she really did . . .

The trial was shown live on television, and had more viewers than popular soap operas. Pam's cool demeanour in court led one reporter to dub her "the ice princess". One newspaper took a poll of readers on whether she was guilty; the vote was more than five to one that she was.

On 22 March, 1991, the jury was out for thirteen hours; when they filed in, none of them looked at Pam Smart — a sign that they had voted for a guilty verdict. In fact, they had found her guilty on three counts: conspiracy to commit murder, accomplice to murder, and tampering with a witness. (She had asked a boy to give false evidence implying that Cecelia was a liar.) The verdicts were unanimous. Judge Grey sentenced her to life imprisonment without possibility of parole. Pam commented about her lover: "I can't believe Billy. First he took Greg's life. Now he's taking mine."

But for their plea bargaining, the three youths would also have received the same sentence. In fact, the two active participants in the murder — Billy Flynn and Pete Randall — each received forty years, with twelve years deferred for good behaviour — a minimum of twenty-eight years each. JR Lattime received thirty years with twelve deferred.

Like all crimes of passion, the evidence in the Pam Smart case offers us an illusion of understanding what really happened. Yet most of the important questions remain unanswered. If Pam Smart wanted to go and live with Billy Flynn, why did she not simply leave her husband? Why did she want him killed? Was it because she was comfortable in her home and wanted to live there without him (Billy Flynn even testified that she had warned him not to get blood on the settee), or because she wanted the $140,000 insurance money?

Yet even if the answer to these questions is yes, it still leaves the riddle of why an apparently normal twenty-one-year-old should decide to have her husband murdered. What made her hate him so much? Was it his confession of infidelity? Or his habit of spitting beer into her face?

But then, it must be admitted that we are confronted with the same question in virtually every case in this book, no matter how straightforward the motivation appears. Why did Ruth Snyder decide that her husband had to die? Why did Ruth Ellis decide to kill a man with whom she was not really in love? Why did Eric Jones decide to risk his neck by becoming an accomplice in the Minicar murder? Unless every "passion killer" could be persuaded to give a completely frank account of his or her motivations, such questions must remain unanswered.

Equally puzzling is the motivation that led three normal teenagers to commit murder – particularly when two of them were uninvolved with the Smarts. Was it simply the boredom that accounts for so much teenage crime in most wealthy societies? Or a desire to impress one another with their toughness? Or was it simply a lack of imagination that meant that killing a human being was for them as unreal as a television serial? If the latter, then was a life sentence, in fact, the correct verdict?

When Pam Smart began her life sentence, a *FRIENDS of Pamela Smart* newsletter continued to plead her total innocence. But a final comment in Stephen Sawicki's book *Teach me to Kill*, seems to summarize the general feeling about the case: ". . . most people would agree that the boys who killed on the night of 1 May most likely would never have murdered anyone, had Billy Flynn not met up with one Pam Smart . . ."

Chapter Eight

Serial Passion

T he term *serial killer was invented in the early 1980s by FBI agent Robert Ressler, to describe someone who kills repeatedly and obsessively.*

The serial killer tends to choose his victims at random, and the motive is usually sexual, sometimes concealing a hidden motive; the Red Spider it seemed was out for revenge, while Nilsen killed for company. Even more important is the fact he (or she) becomes addicted to murder, exactly as if it were a drug.

Bela Kiss

I n 1916, the Hungarian tax authorities noted that it had been a long time since rates had been paid on a house at 17 Rákóczi Street in the village of Cinkota, ten miles northwest of Budapest. It had been empty for two years, and since it seemed impossible to trace the owner, or the man who rented it, the district court of Pest-Pilis decided to sell it. A blacksmith named Istvan Molnar purchased it for a modest sum, and moved in with his wife and family. When tidying-up the workshop, Molnar came upon a number of sealed oildrums behind a mess of rusty pipes and corrugated iron. They had been solidly welded, and for a few days the blacksmith left them alone. Then his wife asked him what was in the drums — it might, for example, be petrol — and he settled down to removing the top of one of them with various tools. And when Molnar finally raised the lid, he clutched his stomach and rushed to the garden privy. His wife came in to see what had upset him; when she peered into the drum she screamed and fainted. It contained the naked body of a woman, in a crouching position; the practically airless drum had preserved it like canned meat.

Six more drums also proved to contain female corpses. Most of the women were middle-aged; none had ever been beautiful. And the police soon realized they had no way of identifying them. They did not even know the name of the man who placed them there. The previous tenant had gone off to the war in 1914; he had spent little time in the house, and had kept himself to himself, so nobody knew who he was. The police found it difficult even to get a description. They merely had seven unknown victims of an unknown murderer.

Professor Balazs Kenyeres, of the Police Medical Laboratory, was of the opinion that the women had been dead for more than two years. But at least he was able to take fingerprints; by 1916, fingerprinting had percolated even to the highly conservative Austro-Hungarian Empire. However, at this stage, fingerprinting was unhelpful, since it only told them that the women had no criminal records.

Some three weeks after the discovery, Detective Geza Bialokurszky was placed in charge of the investigation; he was one of the foremost investigators of the Budapest police. He was, in fact, Sir Geza, for he was a nobleman whose family had lost their estates. Now he settled down to the task of identifying the female corpses. If Professor Kenyeres was correct about time of death – and he might easily have been wrong, since few pathologists are asked to determine the age of a canned corpse – the women must have vanished in 1913 or thereabouts. The Missing Persons' Bureau provided him with a list of about 400 women who had vanished between 1912 and 1914. Eventually, Bialokurszky narrowed these down to fifteen. But these women seemed to have no traceable relatives. Eventually, Bialokurszky found the last employer of a thirty-six-year-old cook named Anna Novak, who had left her job abruptly in 1911. Her employer was the widow of a Hussar colonel, and she still had Anna's "servant's book", a kind of identity card that contained a photograph, personal details, and a list of previous employers, as well as their personal comments. The widow assumed that she had simply found a better job or had got married. She still had the woman's trunk in the attic.

This offered Bialokurszky the clue he needed so urgently: a sheet from a newspaper, *Pesti Hirlap*, with an advertisement marked in red pencil:

> Widower urgently seeks acquaintance of mature, warm-hearted spinster or widow to help assuage loneliness mutually. Send photo and details, Poste Restante Central P.O.Box 717. Marriage possible and even desirable.

Now, at last, fingerprinting came into its own. Back at headquarters, the trunk was examined, and a number of prints were found; these matched those of one of the victims. The post office was able to tell Bialokurszky that Box 717 had been rented by a man who had signed for his key in the name of Elemer Nagy, of 14 Kossuth Street, Pestszenterzsebet, a suburb of Budapest. This proved to be an empty plot. Next, the detective and his team studied the agony column of *Pesti Hirlap* for 1912 and 1913. They found more than twenty requests for "warm-hearted spinsters" which gave the address of Box 717. This was obviously how the unknown killer of Cinkota had contacted his victims. On one occasion he had paid for the advertisement by postal order, and the post office was able to trace it. (The Austro-Hungarian Empire at least had a super-efficient bureaucracy.) Elemer Nagy had given an address in Cinkota, where the bodies had been found, but it was not of the house in Rákóczi Street; in fact, it proved to be the address of the undertaker. The killer had a sense of humour.

Bialokurszky gave a press conference, and asked the newspapers to publish the signature of "Elemer Nagy". This quickly brought a letter from a domestic servant named Rosa Diosi, who was twenty-seven, and admitted that she had been the mistress of the man in question. His real name was Bela Kiss, and she had last heard from him in 1914, when he had written to her from a Serbian prisoner of war camp. Bialokurszky had not divulged that he was looking for the Cinkota mass murderer, and Rosa Diosi was shocked and incredulous when he told her. She had met Kiss in 1914; he had beautiful brown eyes, a silky moustache, and a deep, manly voice. Sexually, he had apparently been insatiable . . .

Other women contacted the police, and they had identical stories to tell: answering the advertisement, meeting the handsome Kiss, and being quickly invited to become his mistress, with promises of marriage. They were also expected to hand over their life savings, and all had been invited to Cinkota. Some had not gone, some had declined to offer their savings — or had none to offer — and a few had disliked being rushed into sex. Kiss had wasted no further time on them, and simply vanished from their lives.

In July 1914, two years before the discovery of the bodies, Kiss had been conscripted into the Second Regiment of the Third Hungarian Infantry Battalion, and had taken part in the long offensive that led to the fall of Valjevo; but before that city had fallen in November, Kiss had been captured by the Serbs. No one was certain what had become of him after that. But the regiment was able to provide a photograph that showed the soldiers being inspected by the Archduke Joseph; Kiss's face was enlarged, and the detectives at last knew what their quarry looked like. They had also heard that his sexual appetite was awe-inspiring, and this led them to show the photograph in the red-light district around Conti and Magyar

Street. Many prostitutes recognized him as a regular customer; all spoke warmly of his generosity and mentioned his sexual prowess. But a waiter who had often served Kiss, noticed that the lady with whom he was dining usually paid the bill . . .

Now, at last, Bialokurszky was beginning to piece the story together. Pawn tickets found in the Cinkota house revealed that the motive behind the murders was the cash of the victims. But the ultimate motive had been sex, for Kiss promptly spent the cash in the brothels of Budapest and Vienna. The evidence showed that he was, quite literally, a satyr — a man with a raging and boundless appetite for sex. His profession — of plumber and tinsmith — did not enable him to indulge this appetite so he took to murder. He had received two legacies when he was twenty-three (about 1903), but soon spent them. After this, he had taken to seducing middle-aged women and "borrowing" their savings. One of these, a cook name Maria Toth, had become a nuisance, and he killed her. After this — like his French contemporary Landru — he had decided that killing women was the easiest way to make a living as well as indulge his sexual appetites. His favourite reading was true-crime books about con men and adventurers.

Bialokurszky's investigations suggested that there had been more then seven victims, and just before Christmas 1916, the garden in the house at Cinkota was dug up; it revealed five more bodies, all of middle-aged women, all naked.

But where was Kiss? The War Office thought that he had died of fever in Serbia. He had been in a field hospital, but when Bialokurszky tracked down one of its nurses, she remembered the deceased as a "nice boy" with fair hair and blue eyes, which seemed to suggest that Kiss had changed identity with another soldier, possibly someone called Mackavee; but the new "Mackavee" proved untraceable.

And although sightings of Kiss were reported from Budapest in 1919 – and even New York as late as 1932 – he was never found.

In Need of a Friend

On the evening of 8 February 1983, a drains maintenance engineer named Michael Cattran was asked to call at 23 Cranley Gardens, in Muswell Hill, north London, to find out why tenants had been unable to flush their toilets since the previous Saturday. Although Muswell Hill is known as a highly respectable area of London – it was once too expensive for anyone but the upper middle classes – No. 23 proved to be a rather shabby house, divided into flats. A tenant showed Cattran the manhole cover that led to the drainage system. When he removed it, he staggered back and came close to vomiting; the smell was unmistakably decaying flesh. And when he had climbed down the rungs into the cistern, Cattran discovered what was blocking the drain: masses of rotting meat, much of it white, like chicken flesh. Convinced this was human flesh, Cattran rang his supervisor, who decided to come and inspect it in the morning. When they arrived the following day, the drain had been cleared. And a female tenant told them she had heard footsteps going up and down the stairs for much of the night. The footsteps seemed to go up to the top flat, which was rented by a thirty-seven-year-old civil servant named Dennis Nilsen.

Closer search revealed that the drain was still not quite clear; there was a piece of flesh, six inches square, and some bones that resembled fingers. Detective Chief Inspector Peter Jay, of Hornsey CID, was waiting in the hallway of the house that evening when Dennis Nilsen walked in from his day at the office – a Jobcentre in Kentish Town. He told

Nilsen he wanted to talk to him about the drains. Nilsen invited the policeman into his flat, and Jay's face wrinkled as he smelt the odour of decaying flesh. He told Nilsen that they had found human remains in the drain, and asked what had happened to the rest of the body. "It's in there, in two plastic bags," said Nilsen, pointing to a wardrobe.

In the police car, the Chief Inspector asked Nilsen whether the remains came from one body or two. Calmly, without emotion, Nilsen said: "There have been fifteen or sixteen altogether."

At the police station, Nilsen – a tall man with metal rimmed glasses – seemed eager to talk. (In fact, he proved to be something of a compulsive talker, and his talk overflowed into a series of school exercise books in which he later wrote his story for the use of Brian Masters, a young writer who contacted him in prison.) He told police that he had murdered three men in the Cranley Gardens house – into which he moved in the autumn of 1981 – and twelve or thirteen at his previous address, 195 Melrose Avenue, Cricklewood.

The plastic bags from the Muswell Hill flat contained two severed heads, and a skull from which the flesh had been stripped – forensic examinaation revealed that it had been boiled. The bathroom contained the whole lower half of a torso, from the waist down, intact. The rest was in bags in the wardrobe and in the tea chest. At Melrose Avenue, thirteen days and nights of digging revealed many human bones, as well as a cheque book and pieces of clothing.

The self-confessed mass murderer – he seemed to take a certain pride in being "Britain's biggest mass murderer" – was a Scot, born at Fraserburgh on 23 November 1945. His mother, born Betty Whyte, married a Norwegian soldier named Olav Nilsen in 1942. It was not a happy marriage; Olav was seldom at home, and was drunk a great deal; they were divorced seven years after their marriage. In 1954, Mrs Nilsen married again and became Betty Scott. Dennis grew up in the house of his grandmother and grandfather, and was immensely attached to his grandfather, Andrew Whyte, who became a father substitute. When Nilsen was seven, his grandfather died and his mother took Dennis in to see the corpse. This seems to have been a traumatic experience; in his prison notes he declares "My troubles started there." The death of his grandfather was such a blow that it caused his own emotional death, according to Nilsen. Not long after this, someone killed the two pigeons he kept in an air raid shelter, another severe shock. His mother's remarriage when he was nine had the effect of making him even more of a loner.

In 1961, Nilsen enlisted in the army, and became a cook. It was during this period tht he began to get drunk regularly, although he remained a loner, avoiding close relationships. In 1972 he changed the life of a soldier for that of a London policeman, but disliked the relative lack of freedom — compared to the army — and resigned after only eleven months. He became a security guard for a brief period, then a job-interviewer for the Manpower Services Commission.

In November 1975, Nilsen began to share a north London flat — in Melrose Avenue — with a young man named David Gallichan, ten years his junior. Gallichan was later to insist that there was no homosexual relationship, and this is believable. Many heterosexual young men would later accept Nilsen's offer of a bed for the night, and he would make no advances, or accept a simple "No" without resentment. But in May 1977, Gallichan decided he could bear London no longer, and accepted a job in the country. Nilsen was furious; he felt rejected and deserted. The break-up of the relationship with Gallichan — whom he had always dominated — seems to have triggered the homicidal violence that would claim fifteen lives.

The killings began more than a year later, in December 1978. Around Christmas, Nilsen picked up a young Irish labourer in the Cricklewood Arms, and they went back to his flat to continue drinking. Nilsen wanted him to stay over the New Year but the Irishman had other plans. In a note he later wrote for his biographer Brian Masters, Nilsen gives as his motive for this first killing that he was lonely and wanted to spare himself the pain of separation. In another confession he also implies that he has no memory of the actual killing. Nilsen strangled the unnamed Irishman in his sleep with a tie. Then he undressed the body and carefully washed it, a ritual he observed in all his killings. After that he placed the body under the floorboards where – as incredible as it seems – he kept it until the following August. He eventually burned it on a bonfire at the bottom of the garden, burning some rubber at the same time to cover the smell.

In November 1979, Nilsen attempted to strangle a young Chinaman who had accepted his offer to return to the flat; the Chinaman escaped and reported the attack to the police. But the police believed Nilsen's explanation that the Chinaman was trying to "rip him off" and decided not to pursue the matter.

The next murder victim was a twenty-three-year-old Canadian called Kenneth James Ockendon, who had completed a technical training course and was taking a holiday before starting his career. He had been staying with an uncle and aunt in Carshalton after touring the Lake District. He was not a homosexual, and it was pure bad luck that he got into conversation with Nilsen in the Princess Louise in High Holborn around 3 December 1979. They went back to Nilsen's flat, ate ham, eggs and chips, and bought £20 worth of alcohol. Ockendon watched television, then listened to rock music on Nilsen's hi-fi system. Then he sat listening to music wearing earphones, watching television at the same time. This may have been what cost him his life; Nilsen liked to talk, and probably felt "rejected". "I thought bloody good guest this . . ." And sometime after midnight, while Ockendon was still wearing the head-phones, he strangled him with a flex. Ockendon was so drunk that he put up no struggle. And Nilsen was also so drunk that after the murder, he sat down, put on the headphones, and went on playing music for hours. When he tried to put the body under the floorboards the next day, rigor mortis had set in and it was impossible. He had to wait until the rigor had passed. Later, he dissected the body. Ockendon had large quantities of Canadian money in his moneybelt, but Nilsen tore this up. The rigorous Scottish upbringing would not have allowed him to steal.

Nilsen's accounts of the murders are repetitive, and make them sound mechanical and almost identical. The third victim in May 1980, was a sixteen-year-old butcher named Martyn Duffey, who was also strangled and placed under the floorboards. Number four was a twenty-six year old Scot named Billy Sutherland – again strangled in his sleep with a tie and placed under the floorboards. Number five was an unnamed Mexican or Philipino, killed a few months later. Number six was an Irish building worker. Number seven was an undernourished down-and-out picked up in a doorway. (He was burned on the bonfire all in one piece.) The next five victims, all unnamed, were killed equally casually between late 1980 and late 1981. Nilsen later insisted that all the murders had been without sexual motivation – a plea that led Brian Masters to entitle his book on the case *Killing for Company*. There are moments in Nilsen's confessions when it sounds as if, like so many serial killers, he felt as if he was being taken over by a Mr Hyde personality or possessed by some demonic force.

In October 1981, Nilsen moved into an upstairs flat in Cranley Gardens, Muswell Hill. On 25 November, he took a homosexual student named Paul Nobbs back with him, and they got drunk. The next day, Nobbs went into University College Hospital for a check-up, and was told that bruises on his throat indicated that someone had tried to strangle him. Nilsen apparently changed his mind at the last moment.

The next victim, John Howlett, was less lucky. He woke up as Nilsen tried to strangle him and fought back hard; Nilsen had to bang his head against the headrest of the bed to subdue him. When he realized Howlett was still breathing, Nilsen drowned him in the bath. He hacked up the body in the bath, then boiled chunks in a large pot to make them easier to dispose of. (He also left parts of the body out in plastic bags for the dustbin men to take away.)

In May 1982, another intended victim escaped – a drag-artiste called Carl Stottor. After trying to strangle him, Nilsen placed him in a bath of water, but changed his mind and allowed him to live. When he left the flat, Stottor even agreed to meet Nilsen again – but decided not to keep the appointment. He decided not to go to the police.

The last two victims were both unnamed, one a drunk and one a drug-addict. In both cases, Nilsen claims to be unable to remember the actual killing. Both were dissected, boiled and flushed down the toilet. It was after this second murder – the fifteenth in all – that the tenants complained about blocked drains, and Nilsen was arrested.

The trial began on 24 October 1983, in the same court where Peter Sutcliffe had been tried two years earlier. Nilsen was charged with six murders and two attempted murders, although he had confessed to fifteen murders and seven attempted murders. He gave the impression that he was enjoying his moment of glory. The defence pleaded diminished responsibility, and argued that the charge should be reduced to manslaughter. The jury declined to accept this, and on 4 November 1983, Nilsen was found guilty by a vote of 10 to 2, and sentenced to life imprisonment.

Lucian Staniak, the "Red Spider"

For criminologists, one of the most frustrating things about the Iron Curtain was that it was virtually impossible to learn whether its police were facing the same types of crimes as in the west. But in the late 1960s, accounts of the "Red Spider" case made it clear that communist regimes also spawned serial killers.

In July 1964, the communist regime in Poland was getting prepared to celebrate the twentieth anniversary of the liberation of Warsaw by Russian troops; a great parade was due to take place in Warsaw on the 22nd. On the 4 July the editor of *Przeglad Polityczny*, the Polish equivalent of *Pravda*, received an anonymous letter in spidery red handwriting: "There is no happiness without tears, no life without death. Beware! I am going to make you cry." Marian Starzynski thought the anonymous writer had him in mind, and requested police protection. But on the day of the big parade, a seventeen-year-old blonde, Danka Maciejowitz, failed to arrive home from a parade organized by the School of Choreography and Folklore in Olsztyn, one hundred and sixty miles north of Warsaw. The next day, a gardener in the Olsztyn Park of Polish Heroes discovered the girl's body in some shrubbery. She had been stripped naked and raped, and the lower part of her body was covered with Jack-the-Ripper-type mutilations. And the following day, the 24th, another red-ink letter was delivered to *Kulisy*, a Warsaw newspaper: "I picked a juicy flower in Olsztyn and I shall do it again somewhere else, for there is no holiday without a funeral." Analysis of the ink showed that it had been made by dissolving red art paint in turpentine.

On 16 January 1965, the Warsaw newspaper *Zycie Warsawy* published the picture of a pretty sixteen-year-old girl, Aniuta Kaliniak, who had been chosen to lead a parade of students in another celebration rally the following day. She left her home in Praga, an eastern suburb of

Warsaw, and crossed the river Vistula to reach the parade. Later, she thumbed a lift from a lorry driver, who dropped her close to her home at a crossroads. The day after the parade, her body was found in a basement in a leather factory opposite her home. The killer had removed a grating to get in. The crime had obviously been carefully planned. He had waited in the shadows of the wall, and cut off her cry with a wire noose drooped over her head. In the basement, he had raped her, and left a six-inch spike sticking in her sexual organs (an echo of the Boston Strangler). While the search went on, another red-ink letter advised the police where to look for her body.

Olsztyn and Warsaw are one hundred and sixty miles apart, this modern Ripper differed from his predecessor in not sticking to the same area. Moreover, like Klaus Gosmann he was a man with a strong dramatic sense: the selection of national holidays for his crimes, the letter philosophising about life and death.

The Red Spider — as he had come to be known, from his spidery writing — chose All Saints day, 1 November, for his next murder, and Poznan, one hundred and twenty-four miles west of Warsaw, as the site. A young, blonde hotel receptionist Janka Popielski, was on her way to look for a lift to a nearby village, where she meant to meet her boyfriend. Since it was a national holiday, the freight terminal was almost deserted. Her killer pressed a chloroform-soaked bandage over her nose and mouth. Then he removed her skirt, stockings and panties, and raped her behind a packing shed. After this, he killed her with a screwdriver. The mutilations were so thorough and revolting that the authorities suppressed all details. The Red Spider differed from many sex killers in apparently being totally uninterested in the upper half of his victims. Janka was stuffed into a packing case, where she was discovered an hour later. The police swooped on all trains and buses leaving Poznan, looking for a man with bloodstained clothes; but they failed to find one. The next day, the Poznan newspaper *Courier Zachodni* received one of the now-notorious letters in red ink, containing a quotation from Stefan Zeromsky's national epic *Popioly* (1928): "Only tears of sorrow can wash out the stain of shame; only pangs of suffering can blot out the fires of lust."

May Day, 1966, was both a communist and a national holiday. Marysia Galazka, seventeen, went out to look for her cat in the quiet suburb of Zoliborz, in northern Warsaw. When she did not return, her father went out to look for her. He found her lying in the typical rape position, with her entrails forming an abstract pattern over her thighs, in a tool shed behind the house. Medical evidence revealed that the killer had raped her before disembowelling her.

Major Ciznek, of the Warsaw Homicide Squad, was in charge of the case, and he made a series of deductions. The first was that the Red Spider was unlikely to confine himself to his well-publicized murders on national holidays. Such killers seek victims when their sexual desire is at maximum tension, not according to some preconceived timetable. Ciznek examined evidence of some fourteen other murders that had taken place since the first one in April 1964, one each in Lublin, Radom, Kielce, Lodz, Bialystock, Lomza, two in Bydgoszcz, five in the Poznan district. All places were easily reached by railway; the *modus operandi* was always the same. Every major district of Poland within two hundred and forty-eight miles of Warsaw was covered. Ciznek stuck pins in a map and examined the result. It looked as if Warsaw might be the home of the killer, since the murders took place all round it. But one thing was noticeable. The murders extended much farther south than north, and there were also more of them to the south. It rather looked as if the killer had gone to Bialystock, Lomza and Olsztyn as a token gesture of extending his boundaries. Assuming, then, that the killer lived somewhere south of Warsaw, where would this be most likely to be? There were five murders in the Poznan district, to the west of Warsaw. Poznan is, of course, easily reached from Warsaw. But where in the south could it be reached from just as easily? Cracow was an obvious choice. So was Katowice, twenty miles or so from Cracow. This town was also at the centre of a network of railway lines.

On Christmas Eve, 1966, Cracow was suddenly ruled out as a possibility. Three service men getting on a train between Cracow and Warsaw looked into a reserved compartment and found the half naked and mutilated corpse of a girl on the floor. The leather miniskirt had been slashed to pieces; so had her abdomen and thighs. The servicemen notified the guard, and a message was quickly sent to Warsaw, who instructed the traindriver to go straight through to Warsaw, non-stop, in case the killer managed to escape at one of the intervening stations. A careful check of passengers at Warsaw revealed no one stained with blood or in any way suspicious. But the police were able to locate the latest letter from the killer, dropped into the post slot of the mail van on top of all the others. It merely said: "I have done it again," and was addressed to *Zycie Warsawy*. It looked as if the Red Spider had got off the train in Cracow, after killing the girl, and dropped the letter into the slot.

The girl was identified as Janina Kozielska, of Cracow. And the police recalled something else: another girl named Kozielska had been murdered in Warsaw in 1964. This proved to be Janina's sister Aniela. For Ciznek, this ruled out Cracow as the possible home of the killer. For he would be likely to avoid his home territory. Moreover, there surely had to be some connection between the murders of two sisters . . . The compartment on the Cracow-Warsaw train had been booked over the telephone by a man who said his name was Stanislav Kozielski, and that his wife would pick up the tickets. Janina had paid 1,422 zloty for them — about twenty-five pounds. Janina had come to the train alone and been shown to her compartment by the ticket inspector. She said that her husband would be joining her shortly. The inspector had also checked a man's ticket a few moments later, but could not recall the man. It was fairly clear, then, that the Red Spider knew the girl well enough to persuade her to travel with him as his wife, and had probably paid for the ticket. He had murdered her in ten minutes or so, and then hurried off the train.

Ciznek questioned the dead girl's family. They could not suggest who might have killed their daughter, but they mentioned that she sometimes worked as a model – as her sister had. She worked at the School of Plastic Arts and at a club called The Art Lovers Club.

Ciznek recollected that the red ink was made of artist's paint dissolved in turpentine and water; this looked like a lead.

The Art Lovers Club proved to have one hundred and eighteen members. For an Iron Curtain country, its principles were remarkably liberal; many of its members painted abstract, tachiste and pop-art pictures. Most of them were respectable professional men – doctors, dentists, officials, newspapermen. And one of them came from Katowice. His name was Lucian Staniak, and he was a twenty-six-year-old translator who worked for the official Polish publishing house. Staniak's business caused him to travel a great deal – in fact, he had bought an *ulgowy bilet*, a train ticket that enabled him to travel anywhere in Poland.

Ciznek asked if he could see Staniak's locker. It confirmed his increasing hope that he had found the killer. It was full of knives – used for painting, the club manager explained. Staniak daubed the paint on with a knife blade. He liked to use red paint. And one of his paintings, called "The Circle of Life", showed a flower being eaten by a cow, the cow being eaten by a wolf, the wolf being shot by a hunter, the hunter being killed by a car driven by a woman, and the woman lying with her stomach ripped open in a field, with flowers sprouting from her body.

Ciznek now knew he had his man, and he telephoned the Katowice police. They went to Staniak's address at 117 Aleje Wyzwolenia, but found no one at home. In fact, Staniak was out committing another murder — his last. It was a mere month after the train murder — 31 January 1967 — but he was impatient at the total lack of publicity given to the previous murder. So he took Bozhena Raczkiewicz, an eighteen-year-old student from the Lodz Institute of Cinematographic Arts, to a shelter built at the railway station for the use of stranded overnight travellers, and there stunned her with a vodka bottle. In accordance with his method when in a hurry, he cut off her skirt and panties with his knife. He had killed her in a few minutes between 6 o'clock and 6.25. The neck of the broken bottle had a clear fingerprint on it.

Staniak was picked up at dawn the next day; he had spent the night getting drunk. His fingerprints matched those on the bottle. He was a good-looking young man of twenty-six. And when he realized that there was no chance of escape, he confessed fully to twenty murders. He told the police that his parents and sister had been crossing an icy road when they were hit by a skidding car, being driven too fast by the young wife of a Polish Air Force pilot. The girl had been acquitted of careless driving. Staniak had seen the picture of his first victim in a newspaper, and thought she looked like the wife of the pilot; this was his motive in killing her. He had decided against killing the wife of the pilot because it would be traced back to him.

Sentenced to death for six of the murders — the six described here — Staniak was later reprieved and sent to the Katowice asylum for the criminally insane.